The Six Pillars of Honest Politics:
And the Power of the Pre-Partisan

♦ ♦ ♦

John C. Rankin

TEI Publishing House
West Simsbury, Connecticut
www.johnrankin.org; www.teii.org

Cover design by Stuart J. Rankin and David R. Clarkin.

First Printing, January, 2008.
Second and Third Printings, February, 2008.
Fourth Printing and edit, February, 2011.
Fifth Printing and edit, June, 2011.
Sixth Printing and edit, October, 2011.
Seventh Printing and edit, August, 2012

Content

Introduction

There is the need for biblical theology to address politics, and this is a workbook for those so interested. This book follows the foundation set in *The Six Pillars of Biblical Power: Real Theology for the Grass Roots*, with the centrality of *the chosen absence of the biological father* and *sorcery at the right hand of power*; and it needs the strategy set forth in *Jesus, in the Face of His Enemies: A Paradigm Shift for Overturning Politics as Usual*. Here, there are four ideas for consideration:

1. First, *the six pillars of honest politics* start with our unique national identity and foundation – *unalienable rights* given by the Creator that belong to all people equally – life, liberty, property and thus, the power to pursue happiness. Under the second unalienable right, this means that the intrinsic nature of the Gospel advances religious, political and economic liberty for all people equally.

2. Second, these pillars serve *a level playing field* for all ideas to be heard equally, and by definition, are *pre-partisan* in nature.

3. Third, these pillars serve *checks and balances on power* in government, according to the consent of the governed.

4. And fourth is the sharp application of *Occam's razor*, to "reduce needless redundancies," or to "keep it simple." Here I propose a model for a simplified state constitution and likewise for the U.S. Constitution, to cut state laws and the U.S. Code by well over 99 percent, and to provide an international template as well.

The biblical definition of a level playing field is rooted in the reality of first being "pre-partisan" so that all honest partisan ideas can be expressed. As a minister of the Gospel, I do not want one inch of greater liberty to say what I believe than the freedom I first honor for those who disagree with me.

We all have our partisan convictions on a range of theological and political issues – ideas we hold with conviction, ideas that differ strongly from the partisan ideas of other people. How do we communicate across such barricades of difference? The very language of being a "partisan" is viewed as negative. Yet I believe it is a good word, if by being partisan we agree to be pre-partisan first, desiring all partisan ideas to be equally heard, confident we are in pursuit of truth.

But at the same time, we cannot pretend to be "objective" observers, to try and keep our "subjective" perspectives at bay. It is not possible to be "non-partisan" unless we also want to be non-human, and the same is true with the notion of being "bi-partisan."

As honest participants in political life, we should openly put our deepest partisan beliefs on the table up front, and clearly for all to examine. This simple act then allows the most crucial question to be posed of all partisans in a free nation, namely, do our partisan ideas provide for the freedom for other partisan ideas to challenge ours? To say yes to this question is to express confidence that we are truth seekers.

Part of such confidence lies in the power of being proactive, or positive. For example, how often are our theological or political ideas merely reactions to other ideas, which are reactions to prior reactions, tracing back to a litany of prior injustices into distant memory? Reactions to reactions only produce an increasingly toxic soup in which we will all miserably drown together, unless the cycle can be broken.

To be truly proactive is a question of origins, and it sets the table for reality. In terms of reality, first is the proactive then the reactive; first is the positive before the negative can exist; and first is the light before the darkness is defined; and in terms of political language, first is the pre-partisan as the basis for the honest partisan, and against both the post-partisan chafes.

The biblical worldview is unique in its proactive starting point, our common historical origin, the predicate for reality, and against which all reactions are measured. In so doing, it is not a formal creed or doctrine that is my focus, but ethics which prove to be universal. These ethics are both pre-partisan and honestly partisan at the same time.

"Ethics," rooted in the Greek terms *ethos* and *ethikos*, is a word that refers to how we treat people. Biblically, ethics are summed up in loving God with our whole being, and thus loving all our neighbors as ourselves. The Golden Rule that flows out of this, and as taught by Jesus, it is proactive – treat others as you wish to be treated.

The proactive also proves to be simple, true and beautiful, consistent with Occam's razor "to reduce needless redundancies" and where the simplest explanation is usually the truest one.

And by the simple I do not mean the simplistic. As the greatest complexities of advanced mathematical theory require the simple fundamental equation of $1 + 1 = 2$ as an assumption, so too in theology and politics we can define one simple interpretive handle for all possibilities – give and it will be given. In mathematics, $1 + 1 = 2$, and interprets all. In theology and politics, "give and it will be given" interprets all, and the six pillars serve such life-giving simplicity.

My goal is to define and create a level playing field for all partisan ideas to be heard equally, in order to distinguish the proactive from the reactive. I can only do this if I am truly proactive, giving 100 percent of my best with no strings attached, held accountable to being proactive by all others, and able to define and test simple interpretive handles for an open and honest political life.

American political life is presently in a death spiral, drowning in a sea of increasingly complex laws. There is an assault against the unalienable rights of life, liberty and property, orchestrated by the top-down god-state. Can we take Occam's razor, rooted in the proactive, and cut out all the reactive elements? Can we cut out the metastasizing cancer of distrust, and restore the health of trust and simplicity throughout our common political life?

Samuel in the Face of Saul

In these pages, and in my assumptions, I seek to be consistently biblical. Yet, there is also a great debate within the communities of biblically committed Jews and Christians: How do we best and most faithfully interpret the Bible as to its political implications today? Writing as a Christian, I include Jews at this point, in honoring the rootedness of my faith in "our father Abraham" – at the merge and overlap of lineal and spiritual realities. Namely, the only theoretical difference between a biblically committed Jew and a biblically committed Christian is the question of the Messiah's identity. Apart from that, it should be the same biblical ethics we both claim.

So, for example, there is a tradition within the Christian church of citing the Hebrew prophets when it comes to a just social order. This is seen especially in the black churches, in "liberal" circles, and in "progressive" evangelical contexts. Yet, too often, biblical passages or verses are treated as isolated proof texts for presuppositional and penultimate political agendas. This is de facto "first politics, then the Gospel in a supporting role," and thus, the opposite of my commitment to "first the Gospel, then politics …"

A well known example is the quoting of the prophet Amos: "But let justice roll like a river, righteousness like a never failing stream" (5:24). Amen. This is a beautiful and powerful metaphor, magnified in the parallelistic poetic structure of the Hebrew sentence, and it easily captures the imagination of heart and mind. And for those who experience the denial or non-opportunity of justice, they await its possibility.

However, in the next breath, many who cite this verse then make a great leap of assumption that, therefore, human government is the necessary remedy to the lack of justice and righteousness. It is assumed that human government should deliver justice through some form of fiat, top-down authority, the passing of laws, and imposition of greater taxes on the prosperous, and thus, the channeling of those taxes for the sake of the needy.

This is large territory, and my purpose here is focused – to question such an interpretive leap. Namely, can such a view be justified from the biblical text itself? The prophet Amos was exhorting ancient Israel, in the mid-eighth century B.C, for disobeying the Law of Moses, for the trampling of the poor and needy. Exile and judgment was promised for an unrepentant nation.

What is the Law of Moses? And how does it address the basis for justice and righteousness in the social order? What is the proper form of government ordained by Yahweh for the exodus community coming out of slavery in Egypt? Here, let me list some biblical realities, some details of which I write about elsewhere.

1. In the biblical order of creation, it was a covenant of freedom given to Adam and Eve – the freedom to choose between good and evil, and thus, to reap the fruit of such choices made. True freedom is the power to do the good.

2. In the brokenness of this covenant that followed, the Messianic purpose was to restore such freedom through the power of "redemption," a word that means to "but back out of slavery."

3. The central reality of Hebrew identity in the Bible is the exodus from slavery in Egypt through the ministry and Law of Moses. So, for

example, in the giving of the Ten Commandments in Exodus 20, it begins with the words of God, "I am Yahweh your God, who brought you out of Egypt, out of the land of slavery."

4. The Ten Commandments that followed prove to be the summation of a just and righteous and social order, rooted in true freedom. The Law is meant to be chosen, not imposed, as Moses and Joshua both made clear later (e.g. Joshua 24:14ff where the "consent of the governed" is first defined in the history of national laws).

5. After Moses, leadership of the covenant nation was given to "judges" or "leaders," starting with Joshua, ordained by Yahweh as King to govern the 12 federated tribes of Israel according to the Law of Moses.

6. But by the time of the last judge, Samuel, the nation craved a pagan styled king, and Samuel warned them of the dire consequences – top-down taxes and enslavement (read the account of 1 Samuel for the whole story, continuing into 2 Samuel for its follow through – but 1 Samuel 12 and 15 can serve as a starting point for the crux of this conflict of Samuel in the face of Saul).

7. In the era of the judges, Israel had no national capital, no national shrine (the ark of the covenant was not fixed geographically), no national taxes and no standing army. The 12 tribes were united by the Law of Moses, and they gave collectively to support the Levites and priests in their religious duties.

8. This is the opposite of a top-down government, where checks and balances among the tribes was central in the political economy, and as highlighted in the Jubilee ethic of Leviticus 25 and 27.

9. Thus, for justice and righteousness to flow like a river, the means was not a centralized national government with top-down fiat

powers, but it was through the checks and balances on power under the Law of Moses through the local tribes.

10. The contrast is then between Samuel and Saul After Saul's disobedience and descent into the means of witchcraft to hold onto political power, David is raised up as a king who submitted to the true King Yahweh. And through David's faithfulness, and in spite of his sins for which he repented, we come to understand Jesus's claim to be the Son of David who, as Messiah, is the true King as the incarnate Yahweh.

11. The ethics of the founding of the United States follow the model of the judges in the Law of Moses quite remarkably – 13 colonies federating into one national union, under the rubric of unalienable rights given by the one true Creator, where checks and balances on power – through the consent of the governed – keeps us free from concentrated top-down, ego-centric, pagan styled political power.

This territory can easily serve the examination of many Ph.D. dissertations. I believe it is self-evident in the biblical text, and for the assumptions of the Law of Moses, all fulfilled in Jesus, Messiah.

Chapter One

The Six Pillars of Honest Politics

If political life were to be influenced by the six pillars of honest politics, I believe the positive transformation would be remarkable. And they are immediately derived from the six pillars of biblical power. In the Declaration of Independence and the U.S. Constitution, as rooted in the Reformation and the First Great Awakening, we have the basis for truth, beauty and justice in the social order. The starting point for an overdue political transformation in the United States, in order to return us to these origins, is by returning to the origins upon which they were built – biblical ethics as interpreted into political order. Christian believers, beginning with their leaders, can begin with this theological Affirmation:

The Six Pillars of Biblical Power – An Affirmation

1. **The Power to Give.** We believe that the Creator, *Yahweh Elohim*, the Lord God Almighty, our heavenly Father, employs his unlimited power to give to and equally bless all people as image bearers of God. The power to give is modeled in the faithful marriage of one man and one woman, in parenthood, and is the basis for trust in human society.

2. **The Power to Live in the Light.** We believe that the Lord God said, "Let there be light," and there was light. As darkness and the prince of darkness flee the light, we embrace the power to live in the light

of God's presence, open and accountable to all people in all we believe, say and do.

3. **The Power of Informed Choice.** We believe that the Lord God gives us all the power of informed choice, to say yes to the good of freedom and life, and no to the evil of slavery and death.

4. **The Power to Love Hard Questions.** We believe that the Lord God gives us the freedom and power to pose hard questions of him, and of one another in Christian community. This is the power of sanctifying integrity.

5. **The Power to Love Enemies.** We believe that the Lord Jesus loved the world when we were yet enemies of the truth, drowning in a sea of broken trust. Now, as believers, we are empowered by the Holy Spirit to love those who are, at present, enemies of the Gospel.

6. **The Power to Forgive.** We believe that the power to give is restored to the broken world through the power to forgive, purchased in the life, death and resurrection of the Lord Jesus. Thus, we as believers are called to extend this forgiveness to the broken world, by the power of the Holy Spirit, and in celebration of the mercy that triumphs over judgment in the second coming of Jesus.

These biblical ethics find expression in the Pre-Partisan Caucus, with its rootedness in the Six Pillars of Honest Politics:

The Pre-Partisan Caucus

www.prepartisan.us or **www.prepartisan.org**

The Pre-Partisan Caucus (PPC), sponsored by the TEI, seeks to serve a level playing field for all partisan ideas to be equally heard, in pursuit of honest government. It is rooted in biblical assumptions about the universal aspirations for religious, political and economic liberty.

- If you agree with the affirmation below, and wish to register as a member, email tei@teii.org accordingly.

The Affirmation of the Pre-Partisan Caucus

First: *The Six Pillars of Honest Politics*:

1. The power to give affirms that the unalienable rights of life, liberty and property are given by the Creator to all people equally, and leaders in human government should serve such a gift.

2. The power to live in the light means leaders in human government at every level should be as fully transparent as possible.

3. The power of informed choice is rooted in an honest definition of terms in political debate, providing a level playing field for all ideas to be heard equally, apart from which political freedom is not possible.

4. The power to love hard questions is in place when political leaders honor and answer those who pose them the toughest questions.

5. The power to love enemies recognizes that even the harshest of political opponents share a common humanity and are to be treated with respect.

6. The power to forgive recognizes the need to address our individual and societal transgressions against one another, and to work toward justice and reconciliation.

These six pillars are by definition pre-partisan. In other words, they set the foundation for healthy partisan debates over public policy, in service to the consent of the governed. The deepest partisanship is the creation of a level playing field for all partisan ideas to be heard equally, where the pursuit of truth in any and all matters becomes possible. Truth will always rise to the top in an honest process.

Political candidates who live and articulate the substance of these pillars, regardless of political party, and in contrast with those who do not, deserve to be elected. The PPC may be endorsed by any political candidate, regardless of party affiliation or non-affiliation. But the PPC is a caucus, not a political party, and it endorses no candidate or party.

Second: *The Committee on Political Ideas* (COPI):

A Committee is thus proposed to serve federal and state governments as a sheer positive foundation for good lawmaking. It can be sponsored by the executive and/or legislative branches.

- COPI's purpose is to be sure all ideas for political debate are publicly discussed in an open-ended fashion.
- COPI has no lawmaking purposes, but rather serves as an information resource for committees that work on writing law.
- On a chosen topic, COPI receives applications from partisans, prioritizes their testimonies, and works through them until all ideas have been fully and publicly aired.
- Written presentations for COPI are a maximum 2,000 words, presented orally, there is no limit on footnotes and attachments, and

are each followed by open-ended dialogue in all directions until the partisan is satisfied that he or she has been fully heard.

Third: *Cutting Law by 99 Percent and Taxes by 50 Percent*:

Within the COPI process, the PPC seeks to apply Occam's razor ("reduce needless redundancies") to federal and state laws. The truest answer is usually the simplest. In my book, *The Six Pillars of Honest Politics*, a proposed rewrite of the federal constitution and general statutes equals 25 pages, and for a given state, 33 pages. An international template is also available. This serves the maximizing of religious, political and economic liberty for all people equally. Occam's razor is fully pre-partisan in terms of the essence of the Declaration of Independence, the U.S. Constitution, and all state constitutions, the sum of which can be called "pro-life libertarian" in penultimate political terms.

James Madison rightly feared that if laws become too "voluminous that they cannot be read, or so incoherent that they cannot be understood," then constitutional government is in danger (*Federalist Papers 62*). Simplicity and truth serve the pre-partisan, then and now. A thorough COPI process provides the groundwork to return us to the goal of simplicity and truth, make such cuts and set the economy ablaze in service to all people equally.

The six pillars of honest politics serve the power of simplicity, truth telling and transparency. They naturally separate honest politics in service to the consent of the governed, from self-serving political agendas. And out of honest politics flow the healthiest grappling with specific debated issues. When these six pillars are examined, is there anything in them that is not attractive to all people of good will? This is equally true for the atheist who may not like the mention of the Creator, yet likewise seeks to have his or her unalienable rights of life, liberty, property and the pursuit of happiness protected. What other source is there for these rights? Out of unalienable rights comes the freedom for the atheist and all others to be who they are as political equals, under the rule of law in the United States.

The Nature of the Pre-Partisan

1. The redemption of the nation is found in understanding and advocating the *pre-partisan* in contrast to the de facto reality of the *post-partisan*.
2. The pre-partisan rises above the baggage of all other political labels, is intrinsic to biblical and constitutional realities, and is most natural to those who identify as *pro-life libertarians* (which is ultimately the same as that of the Founding Fathers, and Ronald Reagan's conservatism).
3. Pro-life libertarians are the most natural fit for a pre-partisan caucus, as rooted in the six pillars of honest politics – language and substance that has proven above reproach in the sight of all political partisans, and is deeply attractive to the vast majority of the voting public.

Since 1982, my trajectory into public policy ministry has been pre-partisan in nature. This has been intrinsic to the biblically rooted Mars Hill Forum series, and now, my TEI Radio program (www.TEIradio.com). I have yet to engage in partisan politics in terms of active involvement in a political party, or in support of a particular candidate. But I am free to with anyone who embraces the pre-partisan covenant.

Any honest partisan should love to debate opposing partisan positions in such a fashion where he or she genuinely wants to understand the concerns of the opposing partisan. Anything less truncates our representative government, anything less reflects a loss of conviction that our own partisan positions have and seek integrity. And honest partisan debate is only possible when we first agree on a pre-partisan basis for doing so.

When I first heard Barack Obama's use the language of post-partisan, I was a bit miffed. What did he mean by it? That somehow he was going to get past partisan political debate? I had never heard the term before, yet for years I had been using the language of pre-partisan.

To be *pre-partisan* is ultimately a theological question, and with dynamic political implications. It is rooted in the proactive nature of the biblical order of creation, where an honest definition of terms allows us to choose between good and evil, life and death, freedom and slavery.

By definition, in political terms, the pre-partisan precedes and serves the *partisan*. Honest partisanship is a good, and is intrinsic to the nature of checks and balances in a free and vital society. We all have our partisan ideas, and they need to be debated openly.

But too, partisan is a pejorative for so many people. It makes them think of blind and biased opinions, only in service to agendas found within competing ego-turfs. *Non-partisan* is little better, so often being a convenient cover for partisan agendas, and too, non-partisan is non-human. We all have opinions, and that is a vital part of being human. And *bi-partisan* is of less value yet – a stand-off until one partisan position can gain the upper hand.

By definition, the post-partisan follows after the partisan. But what does it mean? I see three possibilities, one of which can be positive, and two of which are dangerous.

1. First, the post-partisan can mean a simple appeal to move past petty partisan agendas.

2. Second, the post-partisan can mean that debate is over because everyone agrees, and thus, there is no further need for it. The only biblical possibility for this is the full arrival of the kingdom of God, so such a claim would be dangerously messianic.

3. And third, the post-partisan can mean debate is over because those in political authority say so and insist upon it. This is also dangerous, because it is the opposite of honest debate and checks and balances in representative government.

Thus, the term is liable to misunderstanding. The best way to avoid misunderstanding is by jettisoning the post-partisan altogether, and rooting ourselves in the pre-partisan – a term that is clearly understandable.

And in a simple contrast, by definition, the pre-partisan is an introduction to an open-ended conversation; but by any definition, the post-partisan is a close-ended conclusion.

The six pillars of biblical power are by definition pre-partisan. They set the foundation for healthy partisan debates over public policy, in service to the consent of the governed. The deepest partisanship is the creation of a level playing field for all partisan ideas to be heard equally, where the pursuit of truth, in any and all matters, becomes possible.

As a minister of the Gospel, and a member of the consent of the governed, I am fully accountable to these pre-partisan six pillars, and as they are unpacked in a thousand ways.

Are any of these pre-partisan ethics not attractive to all people of good will?

Two days after the 2008 elections, I hosted President-elect Obama's former pastor, Dr. Jeremiah Wright, in a public forum, where we looked at the question, "The Bible, Race and American History: What are the Issues?" It was a very positive event, even as I disagree with key assumptions in Black

Liberation Theology. I rooted my comments in the pre-partisan, not the post-partisan, organizing my thoughts around the six pillars of biblical power and honest politics. Dr Wright specifically affirmed several of these pre-partisan pillars in response.

Thus, to overcome petty and blind partisanship, we need the pre-partisan, not the post-partisan. This is an invitation for Mr. Obama, and as well, for all political leaders and candidates.

I am a pro-life libertarian, ands this is a penultimate political label I can live with. All political labels are by definition penultimate – bound by the temporal, and short of the kingdom of God. My deepest identity is found in the kingdom of God and the definitive nature of biblical language. The strength of the pro-life libertarian label is that it is rooted in the unalienable rights given by the Creator in the biblical order of creation – life, liberty, property, and hence the power for a socially healthy pursuit of happiness. And as such, being a pro-life libertarian is both pre-partisan and honestly partisan. It intrinsically celebrates the foundation of the nation, and thus, celebrates checks and balances on power, and invites honest partisan debate accordingly.

But too, in our present political culture, to mention the Creator, or dare say, the name of Jesus, even in service to unalienable rights; to affirm man and woman in marriage as foundational for political and social health; to treat women and their unborn as equals; to affirm the idea of limited federal power – all this is seen as partisan by those who believe otherwise. This is fine, and thus I am accountable to competing partisans if they can present superior definitions of the pre-partisan, or why the post-partisan may be superior yet.

I have chosen a label I am glad to affirm, one that is intrinsically positive, one that welcomes all peoples as equals, and one that does not denigrate or pejoratively dismiss those who hold other labels.

But what about other political labels? Are they all not chosen for positive reasons, at least in terms of historical origins?

Conservative means to conserve that which is good. Okay. But, for example, "conservationists," those whose identity is in ecological stewardship, eschew the political term of conservatism. Baggage issues. *Liberal* means to be generous. Okay. But to conserve what, and to be generous with what resources to whom? I like both terms in their original essence, and I am an enthusiastic advocate of a genuinely liberal arts education. But too, how much does "political correctness" (to use another label) sully educational freedom on "liberal" campuses?

How much baggage does "conservative" carry if related to ego-turf protection of incumbent political power? How much baggage does "liberal" carry if related likewise? To speak of "conservative" elements in Russian and American politics in the same breath – are they the same thing? Do "conservatives" in China or Iran have in mind the same priorities as the conservative Ronald Reagan? And I think Reagan's conservatism was in the deepest sense pro-life libertarian in its devotion to unalienable rights and the Founding Fathers as they produced the U.S. Constitution.

Also, the labels of the religious and political *right*, and the religious and political *left* have great baggage, and can be easily manipulated into pejoratives by opposing partisans. Some historical interpolaters say that Stalin was on the "left" and Hitler was on the "right." Yet both were totalitarian. So how helpful is it to use language with baggage if we want to be clear?

The terms *Republican* and *Democrat* are rooted in positive assumptions, in appealing to complementary elements of a constitutional and democratic republic. But too, they are used as pejoratives across the barricades of party politics. They carry baggage, for in both parties there has been intramural debate as to what political philosophy carries the day. To press the pre-partisan into the partisan, the Republican Party presently allows pro-life libertarians in their midst. What about the Democratic Party?

In philosophy, there is a term called *the metaethics of language*. This means that we need to be sure that our language is clearly understood by others, especially outsiders, and more especially, to those who might presuppositionally think they disagree with us.

Here I find the language of the pre-partisan compelling.

Thus, I suggest that all of us who are pro-life libertarians make all other self-chosen labels secondary at the least, if not put out to pasture entirely. If we believe that a pro-life libertarian view is a) biblical, b) pre-partisan and therefore c) honestly partisan, then the "pre-partisan" identity is above reproach in the metaethics of language, and in the face of top-down government partisans. And it will prove exceedingly attractive to the voting public.

Political Theology 101

All people are made in the image of God, and hence we are all equal – we all seek the qualities of peace, order, stability and hope; to live, to love, to laugh and to learn. The image of God includes our calling to rule over the good works of God's creation.

There are four all-defining subjects addressed in the biblical order of creation:

God → life → choice → sex.

Every issue we confront finds its basis in how these four subjects are defined and how they relate to each other, and they equal the content of Genesis 1-2:

God is sovereign, and his purpose in creation is to give the gift of life, especially human life – man and woman as made in his image to rule over his handiwork.

Then follow the gifts of moral and aesthetic choice, and these serve the prior gift of human life. Finally, in the order of creation, is the gift of sex within marriage – here is the power to pass on the gifts of life, choice and sex through procreation to our offspring, to celebrate the height of what it means to be made in God's image.

Or to put it another way, true sexuality is an expression of godly choice that serves the gift of human life that comes from God.

The reversal of the order of creation is thus:

sex → choice → life →/God.

This reversal order is where sex outside the marriage of one man and one woman employs choice to hide from undesired consequences, and some of these choices injure or destroy human life, all in an affront against God the Creator. In the biblical worldview, God is the Creator of life, choice serves life, and thus man and woman in marriage is the healthy definition of human sexuality. The pagan and secular worldviews start with the justification of sexual promiscuity, press choice into its service to cover it up, and where such choices lead to sexually transmitted diseases, concubines, disinherited and orphaned children, infanticide and abortion etc., thus mocking the Creator.

The linkage between the God → life → choice → sex paradigm and the American *polis* is remarkable. *Polis* is the classical Greek term for the city and shared culture, walled off in safety against marauders or armies, and wild animals. From it we derive the English words "politics" and "polity." The Bill of Rights, the first Ten Amendments to the U.S. Constitution, and especially the First Amendment, are rooted here.

The Declaration of Independence gives definition to the concept of civil rights and a limited government with these words:

> We hold these truths to be self-evident, that all men are created equal, that they are Endowed by their Creator with certain unalienable Rights, that among these are Life, Liberty and the pursuit of happiness. That to secure these rights, Governments are instituted among Men, deriving their just powers from the consent of the governed.

In the Fifth and Fourteenth Amendments to the U.S. Constitution, these rights are legally defined as protecting citizens from the deprivation of "life, liberty or property" without due process of law. The word "men" as used in the Declaration can be understood in its best literary sense as inclusive of all humankind – men, women and children. This commitment to unalienable rights as endowed by God has enabled the United States to overcome inherited evils – to thus remove religious tests as barriers to citizenship and public office, and later to legally emancipate blacks, women and Native Americans to receive such rights, at least in principle.

The alignment between biblical ethics and the Declaration of Independence is both explicit and implicit, reflecting an understanding of history and human nature by its signatories. The specific language choice of "Creator" and the Declaration's preceding language of "the Laws of Nature and of Nature's God" assume an understanding of Genesis 1-2, the order of creation. Here, God set forth the natural order, or Nature, as it was intended to be. In the Constitution's insistence on checks and balances of power, it realizes that human sin is a destructive reality that accomplished a reversal of the natural order. And the goals of a limited federal government are to serve the religious freedom and social order necessary for all people to seek a reversal of the reversal insofar as possible in human affairs. In other words, in pursuit of the biblical reality of creation, sin and redemption.

This also equals God → life → choice → sex, and in this paradigm:

God = a parallel to the "Creator;"

life = a parallel to "Life;"

choice = a parallel to "Liberty;" and

(biblical) sex = a parallel to "the pursuit of happiness."

The Declaration begins with God as our Creator who endows us with unalienable rights. The first right is that of life, followed by liberty, which equals the language of choice or freedom. Then the language of the pursuit of happiness, along with that of "property," is set forth in the Fifth and Fourteenth Amendments.

Human sexuality in the order of creation is based on the joining of man and woman in marriage, as equals and complements, where the man leaves his parent's household to join with his wife in order to establish a new household. It equals the completion of the order of creation in Genesis 1-2, summing up these two chapters in how they establish the social order – man and woman in marriage.

The Greek word for "household" is *oikonomos,* our root for the English word "economics" (same concept as the Hebrew word *bayith*). The household, rooted in man and woman in marriage, is the basis for their property rights and economic productivity, which in total yields society's power for the pursuit of happiness. This is the nature of the order of creation, before the brokenness of trust in matters of human sexuality, and thus, redemption is deeply concerned with marriage.

The logic of the order of creation shows the source of the Declaration's use of unalienable rights. In Genesis 1-2, the Creator gives us life, liberty and stewardship over the earth – and the right to receive them as his gifts. No concept of pagan deity or secular philosophy, at their origins, ever approaches this goodness. Unalienable rights for all people are rooted in

Genesis 1-2. The God → life → choice → sex reality of Genesis 1-2 assumes that marriage and family are the social foundation through which God gives unalienable rights. Therefore it is incumbent for us who are Christian to embrace our biblical, our Hebrew, our universal roots, and to be radical in the promotion of civil liberties for all people equally, since we celebrate the very power upon which civil rights are founded. The covenant of marriage – one man, one woman, one lifetime – is central.

Thus, we have some threshold theological context for the six pillars of honest politics, the level playing field and the power of the pre-partisan.

Accordingly, we are all free to define our partisan theological beliefs as they apply to politics. But in so doing, all our ideas and proposals, beginning here with my own, are always open to challenge in the checks and balances of a self-governing *polis*.

I have no interest in law engaging in minutiae, that is, the micromanagement of people's lives from a state or federal perspective where those in top-down power seek to define the lives of others, in all issues, in a one-size-fits-all straightjacket. We need robust debate among equals.

The debate on how to define and implement central political principles belongs at the most local level possible, where people know each other, share common lives and thus, where trust most naturally happens and can be nurtured; then on upward to a limited federal government.

◆ ◆ ◆

Chapter Two
Pro-Life Libertarian Political Platform

The Pre-Partisan Caucus is most naturally suited for pro-life libertarians, but it is not exclusive. Anyone who affirms its three-point agenda is welcome. This leads to a pro-life libertarian political platform, with a more detailed political philosophy defined. Though I attempt to make it fully biblical, there can be honest room for disagreement. And this is why the Pre-Partisan Caucus is prior – a means for such debate to happen productively.

The Pro-Life Libertarian Political Platform

The pro-life libertarian political platform is based on trust in limited government. It is inclusive of any and all persons who celebrate limited government and the six pillars of honest politics. The Declaration of Independence gives the original definition to the scope of civil rights and the nature of a limited government to serve these rights:

> We hold these truths to be self-evident, that all men are created equal, that they are endowed by their Creator with certain unalienable Rights, that among these are Life, Liberty and the pursuit of happiness. That to secure these rights, Governments are instituted among Men, deriving their just powers from the consent of the governed.

In the Fifth and Fourteenth Amendments to the U.S. Constitution, these rights are legally defined as the protection of persons from the deprivation of "life, liberty or property" without due process of law. In other words, these rights cannot be taken away from us by the power of the state, unless first we have taken one or several of these rights away from others.

The word "men" as used in the Declaration is understood in its best literary sense as inclusive of all humankind – men, women and children. It was this commitment to unalienable rights, with the checks and balances on power in the consent of the governed that enabled the United States to overcome inherited evils. Especially, it allowed us to legally emancipate blacks and women to fully participate in our democratic and constitutional republic. And it should apply likewise to Native Americans.

The basis for civil rights in the Declaration naturally follows the biblical order of creation where the subjects of God, life, choice and sex are introduced. In the beginning is God, and his highest goal in creation is human life, as he made man and woman in his image to be stewards of the good creation. Then man and woman are given the power of moral and aesthetic choices. The most important choice involves human sexuality, where in marriage and the establishment of a household, there resides the power to pass on the gifts of life, choice and sex, through procreation, to our children.

The Declaration begins with God as our Creator who gives us unalienable rights. The first is that of life, followed by liberty that equals the language of choice and freedom. Then the language of "the pursuit of happiness," equally with that of "property," indicates the concern for human sexuality. Here, as man and woman join in marriage, they then establish a new household, which is their basis for property rights and economic productivity, which in total equals the basis for the individual and society's power to pursue happiness.

Rooted in biblical ethics, the pro-life libertarian political platform affirms six pillars of honest politics that are universal in aspiration, and an excellent foundation for a healthy political order:

1. **The power to give** affirms that the unalienable rights of life, liberty and property are given by the Creator belong to all people equally, and leaders in human government should serve such a gift.
2. **The power to live** in the light means leaders in human government at every level should be as fully transparent as possible.
3. **The power of informed choice** is rooted in an honest definition of terms in political debate, providing a level playing field for all ideas to be heard equally, apart from which political freedom is not possible.
4. **The power to love hard questions** is in place when political leaders honor and answer those who pose them the toughest questions.
5. **The power to love enemies** recognizes that even the harshest of political opponents share a common humanity and are to be treated with respect.
6. **The power to forgive** recognizes the need to address our individual and societal transgressions against each other, and to work toward justice and reconciliation.

As human life is protected, human liberty is established, and property rights and the pursuit of happiness are made possible.

These three contexts for civil rights equal the scope of a limited government, at the federal and state levels. Their necessary and logical order equals the framework for defining good law.

Life

Apart from a definition of human life, questions of liberty, property and law are moot. The pro-pife pibertarian political platform affirms:

1. All human life is made in God's image, is of equal value in God's sight, and for its entire natural duration, is to be protected by due process of law as the first order of human government.

2. The historic family unit, rooted in heterosexual, faithful and monogamous marriage, and the fullest possible presence of both father and mother in the raising of children, is the basic institution in society. It is based on the power to give and it is the cradle for human life. As such, it deserves unique cultural and legal affirmation.

3. Civil society can only exist when trust exists in human relationships, this is what the power to give yields, and is best learned in the intrinsic nature of faithful marriage and parenting.

4. Life can only be forfeit, after due process, when a person deprives another of his or her life.

Liberty

All liberties are in service to human life, and the First Amendment to the U.S. Constitution sets forth the order of liberties necessary for a just society:

"Congress shall make no law respecting an establishment of religion, or prohibiting the free exercise thereof; or abridging the freedom of speech, or of the press; or the right of the people peaceably to assemble, and to petition the government for a redress of grievances."

The pro-life libertarian political platform affirms:

1. The first freedom is that of religious liberty, and only when it is secured is there freedom of speech, press, assembly and redress of grievances. The "free exercise thereof" is secured as Congress gives no preference to one church denomination or religious organization

over another; as it refuses to establish churches, and as it is free itself from being established by a church.

2. The goal is "free exercise," which is to say that citizens of all religious or philosophical persuasions are invited to participate in the political process according to their express beliefs, to participate on a genuine level playing field.

3. Religious liberty celebrates the enfranchisement of all minority worldviews, guaranteeing the vote to all law-abiding citizens. Majority and plurality religious or political worldviews expect no more freedom to advocate their positions than the freedom minority worldviews have. By the same token, minority worldviews have no more freedom to see their positions morally or legally enfranchised, beyond what they can win through the persuasion of the consent of the governed.

4. For those who by choice, circumstance or the brokenness of adversity do not participate fully or partly as members of the historic family unit, they should be equally free from punitive laws restricting private associations. All persons, however, must accept accountability for the public consequences of their private associations and actions, and in no way deprive others of life, liberty or property.

5. The education of children is the primary responsibility and liberty of parents. As such, government must serve this prerogative, and serve local liberties to define the nature and relationship between private and public education. This freedom of choice in primary and secondary education is the foundation for a vibrant higher education, for this nation's commitment to a genuine liberal arts discipline in all

the sciences, and thus for preparation of leadership in all sectors of the culture.

6. There is a crucial liberty for people to choose their own means of health coverage, retirement provision and other "insurance" and "social security" type needs apart from government mandated means. By the same token, where government means have been mandated in the past, all such promises must be honored.

7. The liberty for citizens to disobey civil government is only applicable when and if the Bill of Rights were to be abridged by the force of a coercive and unconstitutional State power, thus seeking to force citizens to deny their religious or other beliefs in word or deed.

8. An immigration policy rooted in the identity of the United States as a nation of immigrants reflects the power to give; our future identity is rooted in the same power to give that welcomes legal immigrants.

9. In its international role, the United States should model its constitutional freedoms. Wherever religious, political and economic liberties are respected or sought after, the United States is free to join in mutually appropriate relationships. As well, the United States maintains its prerogative for national sovereignty and defense as the best means to be an agent for religious, political and economic liberty within the community of nations, respecting equally the same aspirations of all other peoples.

10. Liberty can only be forfeit, after due process, when a person deprives another of his or her rights.

Property

Once life and liberty are secured, property rights and the pursuit of happiness become possible. The pro-life libertarian political platform affirms:

1. The ownership and protection of private property, to keep what is honesty earned, to buy, sell, and trade based on the same; this is the liberty for all to pursue.

2. The reservation of rights to property belongs first with the people, and then within the local and state jurisdictions that are outside the scope of a limited federal government.

3. The jurisdiction of a limited federal government includes those areas where interstate cooperation is necessary for the common good; such as national defense, commerce and the protection of the environment; as well as the protection of life, liberty and property in capacities that transcend an individual state jurisdiction, or supersede it in concert with the unalienable rights to life, liberty and property.

4. The right for collective bargaining in labor matters, and the right not to participate in the same, are equally necessary.

5. Tax policies must support society's dependence on the historic family unit, must be in fair proportion to government's legitimate needs, must be derived from productive economic activity, and must encourage entrepreneurial ventures and capital formation for businesses and job creation.

6. The ethical commitment and logical order of a free market economy is: "Earn all you can, save all you can, employ all you can, and give away all you can." Accordingly, it is understood that wealth, and the cognate power for charity, are produced by families and workers in

the private sector, not by government. Government serves the free market economy in its constitutional role of protecting life, liberty and property.

7. The support of the historic family unit rooted in the faithful presence of both the father and mother, is the best deterrent to criminal actions that violate persons and property, and the best deterrent to substance abuse.

8. Property can only be forfeit, after due process, when a person deprives another of his or her rights.

The Pre-Partisan Caucus affirms the above principles as a guideline for specific public policies. It believes that the government that governs the least governs the best, and accordingly is committed to reducing the complexity and amount of current local, state and federal statutes as much as possible.

Specific Application

Under the definitions of life, liberty and property, these tightly worded statements give freedom for public debate on a level playing field, and can thus result in much simpler laws. All statements are as proactive as possible, affirming the good, which is to say, trusting that where light shines, the darkness will dissipate.

Thus, debates over such issues as human abortion, same-sex marriage, capital punishment, church and state, minority rights, laws regarding human sexuality and pornography, education, health insurance, civil disobedience, immigration, international relations, war and peace, property law, eminent domain, federalism, labor, taxes, economic well being, substance abuse, and a range of others, find their respective places to be addressed.

So much in partisan politics is marketed as being for or against a certain legislative bill, which may or may not be informative as to where a given legislator stands on the deepest issues underlying the bill. Thus, "congressional scorecards" or "voter guides" can be suspect – they often judge the candidate or representative on politically compromised or fungible language. Let's define the terms clearly on the deepest issues, and once we know where a political candidate or office holder stands, we have better ability to trust how he or she will interpret and vote on sundry legislation. This is the goal of the six pillars and pro-life libertarian political platform.

In essence, these realities translate into what can be called, in the penultimate sense, a pro-life libertarian political position – the best way to sum up the Declaration of independence, the U.S. Constitution and the federalist Papers – all rooted in unalienable rights given by the Creator. Liberty is central. And liberty has a deliberate order where religious liberty allows political liberty which allows economic liberty.

Summation

Rooted in the pursuit of simplicity, truth telling and transparency as a summation of the six pillars, the Pre-Partisan Caucus believes the following eight goals can be realized:

1. The power of a level playing field for all ideas to be heard equally – the truth can then best be understood.
2. The power to maximize unalienable rights for all people equally.
3. The power to build a healthy society rooted in the nature of marriage and parenthood.

4. The power to reduce statutory law by at least 99 percent, and thus reduce the size of state government drastically, while greatly increasing the quality of the government for its essential purposes.

5. The power to cut state taxes drastically.

6. The power of an unleashed free market economy to help the state become the best destination in the nation for honest and creative businesses.

7. The power of an unleashed free market economy to cut health care costs drastically, while greatly increasing its quality and access to all people equally.

8. The power of an unleashed free market economy to set local neighborhoods free to prosper, to build up the middle class, and serve tangible hope and prosperity for the poor and needy.

Simplified State and Federal Constitutions, and Statutory Law

As earlier noted, James Madison stated: "If the laws be so voluminous that they cannot be read, or so incoherent that they cannot be understood," then it does us little good to have an elected government. When laws are too complex for the society at large to understand, then government becomes the playground for various politicians, lawyers, bureaucrats, et al., whose purposes are other than the genuine consent of the governed.

Madison would be horrified at today's political swamp in the United States, and the gathering speed of its death spiral, where mind numbing top-down enslaving complexities serve a self-appointed elitist political class, with their allies. The purpose in chapters 8 and 9 is to take Occam's razor and return to simplicity, the power of trust, and hence, the liberty into which this nation was born and aspired to attain. Then follows an international template.

How to Realize the Political Vision of the Pro-Life Libertarian Political Platform

The first step to realize this vision is to find like-minded people who affirm the Pre-Partisan Caucus who agree with the purposes of the pro-pife libertarian political platform.

Second is to find political leaders who affirm the Pre-Partisan Caucus.

And third, in the face of political leaders who do not affirm the Pre-Partisan Caucus, we need to recruit biblically and constitutionally literate members of the Pre-Partisan Caucus to become candidates and challenge them. We will need to replace political leaders who explicitly or de facto resist the ethics of the Pre-Partisan Caucus, and likewise those who may passively acknowledge it, but will not risk their political careers to embrace it proactively.

The Pre-Partisan Caucus will serve such candidates regardless of their party affiliation, offering educational resources, but will not participate in actual political campaigns. In other words, the Pre-Partisan Caucus endorses no political party or candidate; rather parties or candidates may choose to endorse the six pillars and/or the platform.

The defining partisanship of the Pre-Partisan Caucus, both theologically and politically, is the creation of a level playing field for all partisan ideas to be heard equally. Thus, churches can fully participate politically as well. They will never be asked to endorse candidates or parties, but rather are free to host forums where all candidates for a particular office, and/or other dissenters, are equally invited to be heard. This is above reproach in the sight of the Internal Revenue Service, even in view of the unconstitutional 1954 federal law that sought to restrict the political liberties of pastors and churches. But especially, it is biblical – the power of the level playing field.

Two Wall Charts

In the educative ministry of the TEI , two wall charts have been produced for wide distribution, the text of which is reproduced below.

1. A wall chart for all the schools, libraries, city or town halls, and other civic venues in the state: "What is the Consent of the Governed?" Here, the definition of the consent of the governed is given, then traced from the Magna Carta to Thomas Hooker to the present. The goal is to encourage all people to learn how their government is formed, and along with supplemental data, how they can be involved.

2. A wall chart for churches: "A Biblical History of Human Freedom." Here, the biblical source and nature of God's gift of freedom is detailed, and in contrast with the understandings of other religions and secular ideas. The universal aspiration to human freedom is profiled, and this chart sets the deeper foundation for the consent of the governed.

The content of these charts follow.

What is the Consent of the Governed?

(© 2006 by John C. Rankin and Stuart J. Rankin)

The consent of the governed is the bulwark of American freedom, a risky proposition meaning **the government belongs to the people**. We elect our own representatives, and they are always accountable to us. Without a historically informed understanding of the consent of the governed, the only alternative is a slide toward some form of tyranny. A lazy people cannot be a free people.

Dating to the era of **The Magna Carta in 1215**, the consent of the governed only comes to us through a long and bloody struggle between those who aspire to freedom, and those who cling to tyranny. It comes to us through a texture of uneven yet unrelenting progress, through a growth of checks and balances.

Following the signing of **The United States Constitution in 1787**, **Benjamin Franklin** (1706-1790; and also a signer of **The Declaration of Independence**) was reputedly asked, "Well, Doctor, what have we got – a Republic or a Monarchy?" Franklin responded, "A Republic, if you can keep it." In a strict monarchy, the unelected king has the final say; in a democratic and constitutional republic, the people have the final say through their elected representatives.

The phrase "a democratic and constitutional republic" can be a mouthful, but its precision is important. Democracy refers to the vote of the people, yet we are not a pure "democracy." That would be too cumbersome, having every item in the state and nation always voted upon. Such a pure democracy can only work in small communities.

A more accurate term is "a representative government," which is the nature of a "republic." We democratically elect our representatives, who make the law according to the state and federal constitutions which we have also voted upon. If we do not like how our representatives are governing, we can elect others to take their places, or even remove them sooner by more direct means.

Can we keep our republic? This is always a live question. Freedom is consistently at risk of being lost if we are not vigilant to protect it; indeed, tyrants can be elected by a constitutionally illiterate people. The best way to protect our republic is for all citizens to participate in the consent of the governed. Thus, in service to an understanding of the consent of the governed, here is a thumbnail sketch of a few important milestones along the way.

1215: The Magna Carta

In feudal England the concept of "the divine right of kings" was an assumption on the part of many rulers. The king could rule as he saw fit, claiming that his authority came directly from God, and not from the church or the people. In 1100, King Henry I (1068-1135) issued **the Charter of Liberties** which limited the power of the king.

During his reign, King John (1167-1216) alienated **the barons** in many ways including heavy taxation. Drawing on language from the Charter, they forced him to sign **The Magna Carta** in 1215, giving certain freedoms to the church and freemen, but especially requiring the consent of the barons for any special taxes. John saw this as a momentary compromise, but this "consent of the barons," while only applying to a small class of people, was the thin edge of the wedge for much greater change.

1295: The Establishment of Parliament

The powerful baron, **Simon De Montfort** (1208-1265), called **England's first Parliament** apart from the authority of the king. He became de facto ruler briefly after King Henry III (1207-1272) was deposed in 1265, and expanded the principles of the Magna Carta to include a broader range of those with consent – barons, bishops, abbots, knights and town burgesses.

He was killed shortly thereafter as King Henry III regained power. But in 1295, his example led **King Edward I** (1239-1307) to call for the first representative Parliament that included two knights from each county, two citizens from each city and two burgesses from each borough. King Edward declared: "What touches all, should be approved by all, and it is also clear that common dangers should be met by measures agreed upon in common."

In 1362, a law was passed that Parliament must agree to all taxation, and this was reaffirmed by **The Petition of Right** in 1628. Though the calling of Parliament into session was still subject to the king's discretion, **the consent of the governed** gained momentum. In Spain, while New World natives were being forced to convert, the Roman Catholic Dominican priest, **Bartholomew de Las Casas** (1474-1566), declared that all persons are born free, and that "No one may be deprived of his liberty nor may any person be enslaved." Also, the Jesuit priest **Francisco Suarez** (1548-1617) directly challenged the divine right of kings, allowing for kings to be deposed by the people "acting as a whole."

1517: The Protestant Reformation

In Germany, Augustinian scholar and canon **Martin Luther** (1483-1546) did not intend to start **the Protestant Reformation** in 1517. But it came to pass as he sought freedom to hold his convictions when the church authorities tried to silence him. The religious wars of Europe that followed were one long bloody march toward the consent of the governed.

1620: The Mayflower Compact

When **the English Puritans** came to the New World for religious, political and economic liberty, their November 11, 1620 **Mayflower Compact** set the tone for the British Colonies – a written document where "just and equal laws ... for the general good of the colony" were put in place. **Governor William Bradford** (1590-1657), opposed "Arbitrary Government ... where a people have men set over them, without their choice or consent," instead calling for a "government and governors as we should by common consent agree to make and choose..."

The Puritans had sailed from the United Provinces of the Netherlands, where they had been for a season of exile from England. They found greater freedoms there, but yearned for more, so they sought it in the New World. And **the Dutch**, in founding the New Netherlands and New Amsterdam (later to become New York) in 1609, brought with them the consent of the governed in many ways, antedating the Pilgrims by 11 years.

1638: The Fundamental Orders of Connecticut

Thomas Hooker (1586-1647), Puritan pastor and founder of Hartford, Connecticut, was invited in 1638 to address the new Connecticut General Assembly. He challenged them to create a written document where they who "have the power to appoint officers and magistrates also have the power to set bounds and limitations on their power" for "the foundation of authority is laid firstly in the free consent of the people." This led to **The Fundamental Orders of Connecticut** in 1639, regarded as **the first written constitution since antiquity**. It was the first such time a people wrote a compact to form a government on their own, without appeal to any charter or royal concession.

1640: The Settling of Providence

When Puritan pastor **Roger Williams** (ca. 1603-1683) fled Boston, Massachusetts with ninety freeman, he established Providence, Rhode Island. He provided **the most expansive definition of religious liberty since antiquity**. Williams declared "that the sovereign, original and foundation of civil power lies in the people" and that "such governments as are by them erected and established have no more power, nor for no longer time, than the civil power of people consenting and agreeing shall betrust to them."

1660: Samuel Rutherford and *Lex, Rex*

The Scottish Puritan theologian and preacher **Samuel Rutherford** (ca. 1600-1661) criticized the divine right of kings, and was charged with treason by King Charles II in 1660 for his book *Lex, Rex*, "The Law, the King." Rutherford said that the king is not above the law, which is to say the law is king. This simple concept is monumental – **no one is above the law**. Rutherford argued that "politic society is voluntary, being grounded on the consent of men."

1689: The English Bill of Rights

Following The **Glorious Revolution** of 1688, any action of the king required the consent of the people as represented by Parliament. **The English Bill of Rights** declared: "The election of members of Parliament ought to be free," their proceedings were not to be impeached from without, and Parliament was to be held frequently.

1690: John Locke and Two Treatises on Government

English philosopher **John Locke** (1632-1704) was crucially important to **the founders of the United States**, especially in his **Two Treatises on Government**. Rooted in the Reformation and its interaction with the Enlightenment, Locke emphasized reason and toleration, the equality of all men, and their equal say in government. "Men, being, as has been said, by nature, all free, equal, and independent, no one else can be put out of his estate, and subjected to the political power of another, without his own consent." Locke, an Englishman, wrote most of his work while in the Netherlands, finding religious tolerance there as did the early Pilgrims.

Locke argued that all men have **unalienable rights** given by the Creator – life, liberty and property. "Unalienable" is that which cannot be taken from us apart from due process of law, for its nature transcends human government. The consent of the governed depends on unalienable rights.

1776: The Declaration of Independence of the United States

On July 4, 1776, **The Declaration of Independence** from England was signed by 56 men at the risk of their lives and properties in pursuit of liberty. With their eloquent scribe **Thomas Jefferson** (later also to serve as President), the consent of the governed took central stage at the very foundation of the noble **"American Experiment"** in which we still live today:

"We hold these Truths to be self-evident, that all Men are created equal, that they are endowed by their Creator with certain unalienable Rights, that among these are Life, Liberty and the Pursuit of Happiness – That to secure these Rights, Governments are instituted among Men, deriving their just Powers from the Consent of the Governed, that whenever any Form of Government becomes destructive of these Ends, it is the Right of the People to alter or to abolish it, and to institute new Government."

1780: The Massachusetts Constitution, Declaration of Rights

The state constitutions of the original thirteen colonies also affirmed the consent of the governed strongly. In Massachusetts, **John Adams** (1735-1826), who also served later as President, crafted the most detailed language:

"**Article V** – "All power residing originally in the people, and being derived from them, the several magistrates and officers of government, vested with authority, whether legislative, executive or judicial, are their substitutes and agents, and are at all times accountable to them."

"**Article VII** – Government is instituted for the common good; for the protection, safety, prosperity and happiness of the people; and not for the profit, honor, or private interest of any one man, family or class of men: Therefore the people alone have an incontestable, unalienable, and indefeasible right to institute government; and to reform, alter, or totally change the same, when their protection, safety, prosperity and happiness require it.

"**Article VIII** – In order to prevent those, who are vested with authority, from becoming oppressors, the people have a right, at such periods and in such manner as they shall establish by their frame of government, to cause their public officers to return to private life…"

1787: The United States Constitution

The assumption of the consent of the governed in the Declaration was so strong that the preamble to **The United States Constitution** starts with a bold simplicity, **"We the People…,"** and 42 state constitutions do essentially the same.

In **the First Amendment**, Congress was prohibited from establishing a national church so that religious liberty would not be restricted; thus all subsequent liberties of speech, press, assembly and redress of grievances were able to flourish: "Congress shall make no law respecting an establishment of religion, or prohibiting the free exercise thereof; or abridging the freedom of speech, or of the press, or of the right of the people peaceably to assemble, and to petition the Government for a redress of grievances."

In the Fifth and Fourteenth Amendments, the language of unalienable rights was legally codified: "nor shall any person be deprived of life, liberty and property, without due process of law."

1818: The Connecticut Constitution, Declaration of Rights

"**SEC. 1.** All men when they form a social compact, are equal in rights; and no man or set of men are entitled to exclusive public emoluments or privileges from the community.

"**SEC. 2.** All political power is inherent in the people, and all free governments are founded on their authority, and instituted for their benefit; and they have at all times an undeniable and indefeasible right to alter their form of government in such manner as they may think expedient."

1863: President Abraham Lincoln and the Gettysburg Address

As the consent of the governed grew in its centrality, various people, including blacks, women and Native Americans, had yet to be fully included.

In **The Gettysburg Address**, delivered during the darkest hours of The Civil War, **Abraham Lincoln** said:

"Fourscore and seven years ago our fathers brought forth, on this continent, a new nation, conceived in liberty, and dedicated to the proposition that all men are created equal … that this nation, under God, shall have a new birth of freedom – and that government of the people, by the people, for the people, shall not perish from the earth."

In **The Emancipation Proclamation** of 1863, followed by **the Thirteenth, Fourteenth and Fifteenth Amendments**, black Americans gained consent; in **The Nineteenth Amendment** of 1920 women won the constitutional right to vote; but Native Americans are still not fully enfranchised, as many live in tension between two worlds – the status of theoretically sovereign tribal nations, while also being Americans.

1981: President Ronald Reagan's First Inaugural Address

"So, as we begin, let us take inventory. We are a nation that has a government – not the other way around. And this makes us special among the nations of the Earth. Our Government has no power except that granted it by the people."

If we honor the long struggle for the consent of the governed, then we cannot be a lazy people. We are called to hold those in government to be fully accountable to "We the People" on all occasions. "We the People" means all of us. If we are ever unsatisfied with government, we have a remedy – become involved, and make the consent of the governed a living reality.

What is the Biblical Nature of Human Freedom?

(© 2006 John C. Rankin)

An Invitation to a Banquet: "In Feasting You Will Continually Feast…"

In the Bible, the first words spoken by the Sovereign God to Adam are words of freedom – and this makes the Bible unique. All of humanity yearns for freedom, but how do we advance it in the face of coercion and tyranny?

In Genesis 2:16, almost all English translations reflect similar words: "You are free to eat..."

In the Hebrew, the language is far more robust: **"In feasting you will continually feast..."** [transliterated as ákōl tōkail, being two tenses of the verb "to eat" which equal the force of an active participle – a feast where the feasting never ends].

Thus, the biblical metaphor for freedom is the invitation to a banquet of unlimited good choices. Now, who does not like to enjoy a feast with family and friends? This is the nature of human freedom given in the Bible.

On many occasions, in speaking in Christian churches or to skeptical university audiences, I have defined this language of freedom. And for fun, I have asked everyone there, all things being equal, "Who here does not enjoy a good feast?" Virtually no one raises his or her hand.

In other words, the whole world is united in good biblical theology, whether they know it or not – we all love a good feast.

The verb "to eat," or "to feast," introduced in Genesis 2:16, is one of the most important ideas in the whole Bible. Hebrew holidays are feasts; the Passover is a fast feast for the deliverance of the Israelites from slavery in Egypt; in the book of Isaiah, the mountain of Yahweh is a place of feasting and drinking, and also Yahweh invites the thirsty to come and drink at no cost; Jesus blesses the wedding feast at Cana; the Lord's Supper is a feast of thanksgiving for the deliverance from sin which Jesus accomplished on the cross; the wedding supper of the Lamb is the feast which inaugurates the eternal kingdom of God, where as the redeemed, we all sit down together; in the third chapter of Revelation, Jesus invites us to eat with him; and in the last chapter of Revelation, the tree of life is restored, and the "free gift of the water of life" are the final words of the Spirit to the churches.

Or the Freedom to Refuse the Invitation and Eat Poison Instead: "In Dying You Will Continually Die..."

But freedom by definition is a gift, and all gifts, when given, carry the risk that the gift will be rejected.

The whole text in Genesis 2:15-17 reads this way:

"Yahweh God took the man and placed him in the Garden of Eden to work it and take care of it. And Yahweh God commanded the man, 'In feasting you will continually feast from any tree in the garden; but you must not eat from the tree of the knowledge of good and evil, for in the day you eat of it, in dying you will continually die.' "

In Genesis 2:17, almost all English translations reflect similar words: "You will surely die."

In the Hebrew, the language is far more robust: **"In dying you will continually die..."** [transliterated as mōth támūth, being two tenses of the verb "to die" which equal the force of an active participle – a death that always keeps dying].

In other words, we see a powerful contrasting parallel in the language:

"In feasting you will continually feast..." versus

"In dying you will continually die..."

Two Questions

First, what is the nature of "the tree of the knowledge of good and evil?"

This is a Hebraicism, a way of speaking that includes everything on a given topic within a range of opposites. For example, we recognize this in Psalm 103, where David speaks of our transgressions being removed from us, "as far as the east is from the west." All of space is contained within the opposite extremes of east and west. Or we recognize this in Isaiah 44 when Yahweh says, "I am the first and the last," and when Jesus says in Revelation 22, "I am the Alpha and the Omega, the First and the Last, the Beginning and the End." All of time is contained within the opposites of beginning and end, and the Father, Son and Holy Spirit are greater yet.

Thus, in Genesis 2, "the tree of the knowledge of good and evil" means that all knowledge is located between the opposites of good and evil. And here, who alone can know everything? Only Yahweh God. And who alone can know evil in its totality and not be tempted or polluted by it? Only Yahweh God. Thus, for man and woman to eat of the forbidden fruit is a) to say that God is not good because he is supposedly withholding something; b) to think they can redefine good and evil as they see fit, and hence; c) to think they can make themselves equal to God. The folly of the first sin, sparked by the lies of the ancient serpent, is that Adam and Eve chose to eat of the one fruit which led to death. They thus rejected the unlimited menu of good fruits given to them, including the tree of life, which was given so they would live forever. They became slaves to sin and death, forfeiting freedom and eternal life in that moment.

Second, why does the sovereign Yahweh God allow man and woman to choose death? Why give us such a terrible freedom?

Let's look at it this way: A gift that is forced is not a gift; and love is a gift, but forced love is rape. If freedom were forced on us, we would not be free – we would be mere puppets or slaves. We could not be the image-bearers of God, given authority to be stewards of his good creation. Since God is free, then as his image-bearers, man and woman were made free. Freedom is the power to do the good; but when we do evil, we are no longer free – we are slaves to evil. Only the true and sovereign God is free in his goodness not to do evil. As finite creatures, if we are without the freedom to say no to his gift of freedom, we would be puppets or slaves. To put it another way: Without the freedom to say no, we do not have the freedom to say yes.

Yahweh God is radical [a word which means "root level"]. In the Garden of Eden he gives man and woman **a level playing field to choose between good and evil**. He gives us the power of informed choice, the power to consent to his government or not. He allows the ancient serpent, Satan, access to the Garden to demonstrate the reality of this choice. And the contrast is clear in the Hebrew syntax: Yahweh defines terms accurately as he calls life good and death evil; Satan later defines terms falsely as he reverses reality and calls death life, and life death. **Human freedom depends on an accurate definition of terms.**

Now, had Yahweh God instead given the first man and woman no such freedom, he would have stooped to the level of a pagan deity, to the nature of false gods that rape and enslave, but do not love. He would not be sovereign. But he is the sovereign Yahweh God, the only One great enough to give us the gift of freedom.

The Three All-Defining Doctrines of the Bible

This promise of freedom occurs in the biblical order of creation.

On its own terms, the Bible is the only fully true story ever told. And unless we know its story line, we cannot enter into its truth. That story line can be summed up in the three all-defining doctrines located in Genesis 1-3:

- *Creation → Sin → Redemption.*

Several other ways to sum up these doctrines are these:

- *The Order of Creation → The Reversal → The Reversal of the Reversal.*

- *The Wholeness of Creation → Brokenness → Restoration to Wholeness.*

- *Freedom → Slavery → Return to Freedom.*

Genesis 1 is the grand design of the order of creation, where God, as Governor of the universe, declares everything "good." Man and woman are the crown of his creation, the image-bearers of God. When they are made, and set as stewards of the good creation, God declares it "very good." In Genesis 2, we learn how very good it is as God makes his first covenant with man and woman. A covenant is a promise God makes to us, and he guarantees it will be fulfilled if we accept and honor it. In Genesis 2 it is **the covenant of freedom**, beginning with the words, "In feasting you will continually feast…"

But in the reversal of the order of creation, freedom is lost, and the need is for redemption – a word that means "to buy back out of slavery." In the exodus, Yahweh redeemed the Israelites out of slavery in Egypt; and in Jesus, God paid the redemption price from slavery to sin, offering it to all humanity. In order to serve the reversal of the reversal, we must first know the original order of creation which centers on the covenant of freedom. We oppose coercion and tyranny by living and offering freedom in the name of Jesus.

The Contrast with the Babylonian Genesis and All Pagan Religions

In contrast to the Bible, all pagan religions or secular constructs, when traced back to their oldest known origins, have no sense of a good order of creation. They assume brokenness of trust, murder, war, slavery, promiscuity and tyranny from the outset. Pagan religions and secularism involve people, who like all of us, were made in God's image, made for freedom. But, being distanced from the biblical order of creation, they lost memory of the source and nature of human freedom while still yearning for it.

The most well-known pagan origin story is the Babylonian genesis, and many skeptical scholars in the last 150 years have tried to say it is older than the biblical Genesis. It is not. And these scholars also argue that the biblical Genesis actually derives from Babylonian genesis. It does not. But all pagan religions do come ultimately from Babylonian religion. A brief review can help show the contrast.

At the start of its story line, the Babylonian genesis is chaotic in its description of the original gods and goddesses. A chief god, Apsu, is murdered by another chief god Ea. Apsu's wife, the goddess Tiamat, wants to avenge his death. Then Ea's son Marduk squares off in battle with Tiamat, with an army of gods and goddesses on each side.

Marduk wins, splits Tiamat's skull and scatters her blood to the winds. He then splits her carcass into two halves, and with one half makes the heavens and with the other makes the earth. This makes him the chief god. He forces all of Tiamat's defeated army into slavery, and then they complain about the menial tasks they had to perform. So Marduk killed the god Kingu, who was the new husband of Tiamat, and with his blood created man and woman to be slaves to the defeated gods. Slaves to slaves.

So the Babylonian genesis starts with acts of destruction. But how can you destroy something that has not been already created? The Babylonian genesis has no concept of a good creation, or even a story of how the original gods and goddesses came to exist. Thus, it shows how it comes out of the experience of human brokenness; not the biblical order of creation which truly comes first, which is good and which has no destruction in it. In the destructive story line of the Babylonian genesis, the gods and goddesses are slaves to competing tyrannies and war, and man and woman are made to be slaves to slaves. This is the opposite of the biblical nature of human freedom.

Every other pagan religion cannot rise above the assumption that murder, war, distrust and brokenness have always existed; and though secular thought is rooted in a reaction to Greek religion, it too cannot rise to any concept of a good order of creation.

The Biblical Witness

As the history of redemption unfolds in the Bible, the goal is to restore us to the original covenant of freedom. True government in the Bible is honored when judges, kings and other leaders derive their authority from Yahweh, and thus serve human freedom and the original consent of the governed rooted in the order of creation.

In Deuteronomy 30, at the end of his life, Moses sets before the Israelites the choice between life and death, and calls them to choose life.

In Joshua 24, just before the Israelites entered Canaan, Joshua calls them to choose whom they would serve. Would it be the destructive pagan deities of Babylon, Egypt or the Amorites; or would they, like Joshua, choose to serve the good Yahweh?

In 1 Kings 18, Elijah preaches the shortest sermon in the Bible, calling on the Israelites to stop wavering between two opinions. Choose whether to serve the good Yahweh or the destructive Baal.

At the beginning of Galatians 5, the apostle Paul sums up the reality of the New Covenant – for the sake of freedom, Christ has set us free from slavery to sin.

Across Church History

The Christian church began its first three centuries under the fire of persecution from the Roman Empire, and reasonably honored her biblical birthright of seeking human freedom for all people. But when the church became legalized under Constantine, and banned idolatry and grew more and more identified with the state under Theodosius and Justinian, the church began to impose itself on people – violating her biblical birthright of freedom.

From the Medieval Ages to the Reformation, there was a growing movement toward religious and political freedom. It gathered speed following the Reformation, and found political fruit in the Declaration of Independence and the United States Constitution. Here, religious, political and economic liberty were honored for all people equally, and the "unalienable rights" of life, liberty, property and the pursuit of happiness were rooted in the Creator, the God of the Bible.

The Biblical Ethics of the Consent of the Governed

In the political context of the United States, human freedom is centered on the concept of "the consent of the governed" [see Wall Chart I: "What is the Consent of the Governed?"]. "Ethics" is a word that refers to how we treat each other. The Bible is centered on ethics – how we are to love God, and love our neighbors as ourselves [see Wall Chart IV: "The Six Pillars of Biblical Power"].

The Declaration of Independence celebrates the unalienable rights given by the Creator, including "Liberty," which is the legal language of human freedom, and "That to secure these Rights, Governments are instituted among Men, deriving their just Powers from the Consent of the Governed…"

The Source for the consent of the governed is the Creator, tracing back to the first words of Yahweh God to the first man. **And there are two crucial elements for the human freedom of the consent of the governed: 1) an accurate definition of terms** ("life is life" and "death is death"); and **2) a level playing field for all ideas to be heard equally, allowing truth to rise to the top.**

In the face of coercion and tyranny, are we believers in Jesus seen as those who celebrate the feast of freedom, the banquet of an unlimited menu of good choices? Are we seen as hospitable to the yearnings for freedom which all unbelievers also have? Do we have confidence that such freedom is the most powerful means to allow truth to be understood and embraced? If we honor the biblical nature of human freedom, it is able to transform any culture, and will lead the way to the Second Coming and full establishment of the kingdom of God.

There is no freedom to say yes to the good without the freedom to say no. And when people are free to say no, they are much more likely to say yes. There is no coercion in the Gospel. This is the radical presupposition of the Bible.

Chapter Three
Seven Resolutions

As the Pre-Partisan Caucus organizes, there are seven non-binding resolutions the Pre-Partisan Caucus can place before the State Legislatures and the U.S. Congress. They can go a long way to true definition of terms and hence, the power of informed choice. As well, they genuinely serve a level playing field for honest debate.

––––––––––––

Proposed Resolution #1 for the U.S. Congress and the Legislatures of the Several States:

The Creator, Science and Public Education

We recognize that according to the Declaration of Independence, the concept of unalienable rights is rooted in an appeal to the Creator. These rights, as also enfranchised in the Fifth and Fourteenth Amendments to the U.S. Constitution, are summed up in the concepts of life, liberty, property and the pursuit of happiness.

When Thomas Jefferson, and those with him, composed the words of the Declaration, they needed the moral authority to declare independence from the arbitrary rule of King George III. They needed to define those rights that are unalienable – rights that are above the power of arbitrary human government to define, to give or take.

Thus the appeal was made to the Creator who gives unalienable rights, and to which government is held accountable. The Creator referred to is the God of Genesis 1-2 in the Jewish and Christian Bible, and as appealed to by other religious traditions also.

Since these unalienable rights are crucial for the survival of our constitutional and democratic republic, the question of the Creator and the nature of the creation are equally crucial. Part of the nature of these unalienable rights is expressed in the First Amendment liberties of religion, speech, press, assembly and redress of grievances. The freedom of religion includes the freedom of non-religion to dissent from a biblical worldview within the boundaries of the rule of law. And the freedom to dissent from this dissent is also bound by the rule of law.

Thus, those who argue for a material origin of the universe apart from any concept of deity, and thus reject the Creator referred to in the Declaration, are free to do so. By the same token, those who argue for the Creator and a biblical view of creation are free to do so. And all positions in-between share the same freedom.

Accordingly, in matters of teaching science, religion and origins in the context of both public and private education, we affirm the following:

1. Science and the scientific method celebrate the examination of all theories and facts on a given subject.

2. A biblical worldview celebrates God's gift of unalienable rights, and of science and the scientific method.

3. Honest scientific inquiry, which takes as a presupposition the Creator, concerning the origin and nature of the universe and human life, should have equal freedom in public education to have its theories presented, debated and critiqued.

4. Honest scientific inquiry, which takes as a presupposition a material and/or godless origin of the universe and human life, should have equal access in private and religious education to have

its theories presented, debated and critiqued. This is a matter of moral principle, consistent with having exercised the civil right to choose private education.

5. Honest education always seeks to understand disparate viewpoints on their own terms.

In 1988, I led a statewide non-binding referendum in Massachusetts to place the question described below on the ballot. It would have upended *Roe v. Wade* by its level playing field nature, able to demonstrate a huge consensus concerning conception. It was opposed by a powerful core of elitists and kept off the ballot. Here it is adapted for legislative attention as well.

Proposed Resolution #2 for the U.S. Congress and the Legislatures of the Several States:

Human Abortion and a Process of Informed Choice

We recognize that the U.S. Constitution defines three principal arenas of unalienable human rights, and with a specific order – life, liberty and property. For these rights to be protected, they must be defined.

The 1973 U.S. Supreme Court *Roe* v. *Wade* decision left the beginning of individual biological human life undefined. We believe this matter must be addressed by the nation's electorate. If there is truly no consensus as to the beginning of an individual human life, let it be shown, and the status quo will hold and be strengthened. If, however, a clear consensus emerges, let it be instructive.

The Legislatures of the several States and the U.S. Congress should poll its members to answer the following question, and the several States should place this simple non-binding multiple-choice question on their ballots:

In biological terms, when does an individual human life begin?

Mark a cross X next to the answer you prefer. Only vote for one.

A. Conception [   ]

B. Viability [   ]

C. Birth [   ]

D. Write-in [   ]: specify a different biological term _____

———————————

Proposed Resolution #3 for the U.S. Congress and the Legislatures of the Several States:

Human Abortion and Male Irresponsibility

With regard to the social causes of human abortion, we understand the following:

1. Women rarely if ever plan to get pregnant in order to have an abortion, and rarely do women regard human abortion as an intrinsic good. Rather, women most often view abortion as tragic and undesirable.

2. Most abortions occur in situations where the woman is not married to the man who made her pregnant; or in other instances, where a marriage suffers stress to the point where the husband either leaves the marriage, and/or does not want the child to be born.

3. In most abortion choices, some man is pressuring the woman to have the abortion, whether overtly or subtly.

56

4. In cases where the woman is made pregnant by a boyfriend, if he would support her, especially by means of faithful marriage, she would likely keep the child.

5. Apart from the evil of rape or incest, women who get pregnant out of wedlock are complicitous to one degree or another; however, the man possesses the power to forsake her in her pregnancy.

6. In such instances, the male irresponsibility pressures the woman a) to embrace the courage and sacrifice of single motherhood, usually with financial duress; b) to embrace the courage and sacrifice of placing the child for adoption; or c) to reify and abandon the child to abortion, much as the man who impregnated her has reified and abandoned her to begin with.

7. Abortion is thus the ultimate male chauvinism, where such men regard women as sexual objects, who if made pregnant, are discarded like broken toys, sent off to be aborted, so they can be played with once again.

8. Accordingly, "abortion-rights" do not serve women – rather it is most often a ruse for male chauvinists to trample women and children.

Thus, we affirm the following:

- The equal protection for women and their unborn children will not occur until men start being responsible in their sexuality, and regard women as their moral equals and full partners where sexual expression is reserved for marriage – one man, one woman, one lifetime – and where the responsibility of fatherhood is fully embraced.

Proposed Resolution #4 for the U.S. Congress and the Legislatures of the Several States:

Human Sexuality and Civil Rights

1. All persons hold the unalienable rights to life, liberty and property, and therefore they hold equal dignity and protection under due process of law;
2. The historic family unit, rooted in heterosexual faithful monogamous marriage and the raising of children, is the basic institution in society;
3. There are those persons, whether by choice, circumstance or the brokenness of adversity, who do not participate fully or partly as members of the historic family unity.

Therefore, we affirm:

1. Marriage is defined as the union of one man and one woman;
2. No punitive laws shall exist to restrict private association – whether heterosexual or homosexual; and
3. All persons shall accept accountability for the public consequences of their private associations and actions, and they shall in no way deprive others of life, liberty or property.

Proposed Resolution #5 for the U.S. Congress and the Legislatures of the Several States:

Affirmative Action

There are people in our nation who have suffered racial, sexual and/or class prejudice, and thus, the deprivation of civil rights. We believe the only way to serve them is by the radical affirmation of their equal humanity in the sight of God and the social order.

All human beings are created equal, and thus entitled to the unalienable rights of life, liberty, property and the pursuit of happiness. The government's role is to affirm these rights for all people according to due process of law, and such affirmation should never be to the denigration of other people as a consequence.

Affirmation cannot happen without a definition of what is affirmative. The biblical order of creation gives definition as to what is affirmative, and the Declaration of Independence is based on the same.

The principle affirmation in the order of creation is the power to give, which is the nature of the Creator. In the Declaration we celebrate the unalienable rights given by God. This means that true civil rights are given by the One who has the power to give. It means that human rights are not attained by the power to take from oppressors, but unalienable rights are acknowledged and honored by those who, as stewards of God's image, employ their power to give to others.

We celebrate these rights as preceding the intrusion of human sin and broken trust; and the evils of racial, sexual and class bigotries are manifestations of broken trust. To demand rights from oppressors is to condescend into racial, sexual and class warfare, pitting certain groups against others, in a contest of take before you taken. Negation does not remedy negation, thus any "affirmative action" that participates in this power to take will only further fracture U.S. society.

We need instead to celebrate the power to give and it will be given, as the means for securing unalienable rights for all people. What we need are actions and laws based on the biblical definition of redemption, which means "to buy back out of slavery." It means that we who have inherited blessings that have positioned us for social, educational and financial success, hold an incumbency to be thankful for those blessings. It also means that our talents and resources should be employed as redemptively as possible toward those who have inherited various deprivations of civil liberties.

On this basis:

1. We embrace all proactive strategies and laws that affirm unalienable rights, and we seek redemption of all people who have inherited the evils of racism, sexism and/or classism.

2. We reject all actions and laws that carry with them any negations, such as quotas, and we reject any denigration of groups or individuals who are not in need of such redemptive actions or laws.

Proposed Resolution #6 for the U.S. Congress and the Legislatures of the Several States:

Drugs and Crime

In order to address the relationship between drugs and crime, and to seek a restoration of civil order in this regard, we acknowledge the following truths as a general, representative and overwhelming pattern:

1. It is the absence of responsible fathers that does the greatest evil to growing boys and girls, and this evil has disproportionate affect on the ghettos and its minority populations, especially among black Americans. A responsible father is a man who is committed to fidelity in marriage with one woman, and does everything in his power to love and honor his wife. He is thus a model for his children, so that they may also attain healthy marriages. And even when a marriage breaks down or was never in place, a responsible father still does everything in his power to love, provide for and be a model for his children.

2. With such a breakdown in the historic family unit, many boys become functionally fatherless, and without a father to socialize them properly, they seek ersatz "families," which those outside the ghettos call "gangs."

3. Coupled with high unemployment in the ghettos, fatherless boys have idle time and limited possibilities to earn money. Idleness leads to the pursuit of pleasure in wrong and escapist ways such as sexual promiscuity and getting high on alcohol and drugs. A cycle of despair is created that feeds on itself. And fatherless girls become the sexual adjuncts to promiscuous and abusive boys.

4. Drug dependency is the result for many, and the market for illegal drugs produces an underground economy where gangs stake out various "turfs" they control in the selling of drugs. To protect their turfs, they obtain guns (usually illegally), and when turf wars occur, shootings, maimings and deaths result. In order for drug addicts to gain the money to purchase illegal drugs, prostitution and stealing multiplies, the crime cycle grows and reaches into the suburbs as

well. But those in the suburbs have greater resources to avoid many consequences that the poor cannot.

5. Because specific drugs are illegal or state-controlled, an international black market flourishes, driving up the price for such drugs, and in the process crime multiplies further in order to sustain and protect this black market.

6. Because of these root causes and the interfacing and co-dependent cycles, about one-half of the U.S. prison population is incarcerated on drug charges or related crimes. Not only does this cost taxpayers greatly in terms of law enforcement, but the social and spiritual costs are very high as so many U.S. citizens are rendered unproductive, and unable to contribute to the common good.

7. Thus, it is the poor and certain minorities who suffer disproportionately in this cycle, and justice cries out for a remedy to this escalating evil.

Accordingly, we affirm the following starting points in public policy, necessary to begin redressing the problem of drugs and crime

1. The support of the historic family unit, rooted in heterosexual faithful monogamous marriage and the raising of children, is the best deterrent to drug abuse and crime, and the best place for the healing of the drug and crime wounded.

2. As determined by due process of law, specific drugs may be defined as illegal, but with the maximum penalty being a misdemeanor.

3. All persons who use illegal drugs shall accept accountability for the consequences of their choices, and they shall in no way deprive others of life, liberty or property.

Proposed Resolution #7 for the U.S. Congress and the Legislatures of the Several States:

Recitation in the Public Schools

In the face of the debate over prayer in the public schools, all local school districts are free, if they so choose, to include in their school days a public recitation or acknowledgment of the following words from the Declaration of Independence:

> We hold these truths to be self-evident, that all men are created equal, that they are endowed by their Creator with certain unalienable Rights, that among these are Life, Liberty and the pursuit of happiness. That to secure these rights, Governments are instituted among Men, deriving their just powers from the consent of the governed.

We recognize that the word "Men" as used in the Declaration is understood in its best literary sense as inclusive of all humankind – men, women and children. It was this commitment to unalienable rights as endowed by God that enabled the United States to overcome inherited evils. Especially, it has allowed us to legally emancipate blacks and women to fully participate in our democratic republic. And the same is needed for Native Americans. These words from the Declaration form the basis for the U.S. Constitution's concept of civil rights.

We believe that such a public recitation addresses two equal concerns among the citizenry:

1. It is not a prayer, and it is completely free of any establishment of religion in accord with the First Amendment; and
2. It reflects the historical belief of our nation's founding fathers that human rights are given by the Creator, the expression of which is

consistent with the free exercise of religion in accord with the First Amendment.

We also believe it would be good to have the recitation of the First Amendment itself in the public schools:

> Congress shall make no law respecting the establishment of religion, or prohibiting the free exercise thereof; or abridging the freedom of speech, or of the press; or the right of the people peaceably to assemble, and to petition the government for a redress of grievances."

◆ ◆ ◆

Chapter Four

The Sacred Assemblies for the Unborn

www.sacredassemblies.us

This strategy can literally help tens of thousands of women readily turn away from their abortion appointments, and be directed to a Pregnancy Support Center.

First employed in Massachusetts in 1989-1991 in front of the largest abortion center in the state, Preterm, on nearly every Saturday morning, we saw 200+ women turn away from their abortion appointments by their own choices. Many women went to Crisis Pregnancy Centers, gave birth, and a number found Jesus.

After nine months of this witness and worship, the hundreds of college activists recruited by the National Organization for Women (NOW) stopped their counter demonstrations, since we "were persuading too many of them."

The Brookline Police commended our conduct, and the Boston Globe, other media and the Attorney General could not criticize it.

This strategy is set to be restarted, for in 1989-1991, it engendered remarkable demonic opposition which must always be taken seriously. Along with prayer and worship, the present strategy aims to make a visual presence in front of every abortion center in the United States. The power of our slogan and compelling nature of the questions stops many people in their tracks, and gives cause for reflective thought.

The one slogan we used, on a large banner as well as on signs, had white letters on a green background:

You Have the Power to Choose Life.

The twelve questions we pose, black letters on a yellow background, are:

1. **Aren't You Glad You Weren't Aborted?**

2. **Why Do You Feel No Choice But Abortion?**

3. **Is it Your Choice, or His Choice, for You to Abort?**

4. **How Does Human Abortion Add to Your Own Dignity?**

5. **Might You Regret This Abortion Someday?**

6. **Can Anything Good be Said About Human Abortion?**

7. **Does Good Choice Nurture Life, or Destroy Life?**

8. **Why Does the Human Fetus Fight to Stay Alive?**

9. **Why Does "Feminism" Abort Unborn Girls?**

10. **Can Law or Choice Exist Without a Definition of Human Life?**

11. **Can You Imagine Jesus Performing an Abortion? Why Not?**

12. **Is the Abortion Industry Racist?**

Any form of honest thinking intrinsically advances the Gospel, and sends the devil fleeing. In fact, in 1989, when we first started this at Preterm abortion center, one pro-abortion activist said in our presence to a fellow activist: "These people are more dangerous than Operation Rescue – they are going for our minds."

The Power of the Banner

As an example, on September 30, 1989, I was not present at Preterm, but I received a detailed report from several witnesses to one of the most signal examples of the power of this slogan. At the rear entrance, two volunteers were holding up the banner, with other pro-life volunteers also present. One was Sue O'Connell, a volunteer who with her husband would travel nearly 100 miles from Amherst, Massachusetts, and they were as regular as any of our volunteers. That morning, Sue's eight-year old daughter, Kelly, was also with her.

Sue and the others were positioned on the sidewalk next to the entrance to the parking lot, and from the lot people coming to Preterm would then enter the rear door. There were about eight "escorts" positioned by the door, many dozens of feet away from Sue and Kelly, each wearing aprons designating their escort status. These were women and men, serving as volunteers (I was told) to Preterm, to "guard" incoming "clients" from being harassed by "anti-choice zealots." Since the parking lot was private property, our volunteers never went onto it from their public sidewalk positions.

This particular morning, a college-age woman walked down the street and was preparing to cross the lot to the rear door. As she did, she stopped, looked at the banner and pondered its words. Sue offered her some printed literature, and the young woman was preparing to receive it. But during those moments, the eight escorts saw what was happening and quickly came up and surrounded her, creating a human blockade around her with arms linked. This was a common practice such escorts developed to shield women when trying to break through an Operation Rescue blockade wall. Blockade against blockade, force against force, human angst against human angst. So it was tragicomical to witness their intensity of forming such a blockade where there was no physical interference to such women as they entered the abortion center. But they had a deeper fear – that abortion-minded women might intelligently reconsider their choice, and seek some informed input from a different perspective. Thus, these escorts started shouting and chanting so as to prevent her from hearing anything Sue might say, and especially to prevent any printed literature from coming her way. Thus they forced her into the doors of Preterm by such a surrounding tactic, being careful not to physically touch her and run afoul of the law.

One witness to the event told me that as much as he opposed the tactic of blockade, the sight of the woman being hustled inside made him so frustrated that he emotionally wanted to physically intervene. As he wrestled with these thoughts, eight-year old Kelly O'Connell started praying out loud and with the strength of child-like faith, as she rebuked the devil, his deceit and his influence upon that young woman, and commanded in Jesus's name that she would come out of Preterm. And within minutes the woman did, shaken in countenance, making her way back to Sue and the others, where she received some materials and went her way. A triumph for the biblical power of informed choice. By God's grace, not by answering coercion and lawlessness with opposing coercion and lawlessness – but by answering with prayer.

Thus the banner, in its summation of biblical theology, "You have the power to choose life," has a power that abortion-rights activists are unable to answer. When Yahweh said to Cain that he must overcome his sin, and when Moses and Joshua told the Jews to choose between life and death, between the true God and the false gods, he was saying that they "have the power" to do so. Not the intrinsic ability within sinful humanity to overcome evil, but the broken remains of God's image within them are sufficient by God's grace to discern truth from falsehood, and to say "help me Lord," at which point he sends his help. By acknowledging this "power" within hurting people, we serve the reversal of the reversal, and redeem the language of choice to serve human life, not to destroy it.

The Power of the Questions

Our ten signs (later they became twelve) also proved effective at having women stop and reconsider their intentions, and effective at catalyzing conversations with the abortion-rights activists. I conceived of them the day before our first chorus, and they remained almost unchanged for our entire two years at Preterm, and as we changed them from cardboard signs to more durable materials.

On September 9, 1989, as we began to be present every Saturday, and the numbers of people equaled about 40 on each side, I saw some of the fruit of how deeply these signs affected the abortion-rights activists. A woman representing the "Reproductive Rights Network" ("R2N2" as her signs also said) had taken the time to make six signs, each numbered correspondingly to our signs (as then numbered, as in the meantime I have added a new #3, and the old #3 becomes #4 etc.).

In each case they sought to answer the questions we had posed. I was delighted. She was trying to have other abortion-rights activists hold up her signs, but almost without success. So I went to strike up a conversation with her, and thanked her for having taken the time to answer our questions in such a fashion. I asked her if she were interested in talking about her answers, but she was very tense, distrustful, and did not want to talk. Yet she could not resist asking me some questions, and as I answered, she relaxed somewhat. I then asked her if I could copy down the words from her signs, and she was hesitant, and then allowed me to do so, as long as I did not harm any of her signs. So I sat on the sidewalk and copied their words down:

Question #1: Aren't you glad you weren't aborted?

Answer #1: My mother is pro-choice and I am glad that she was not forced to bear an unwanted child.

Question #2: Why do you feel no choice but abortion?

No Answer:

Question #3: How does human abortion add to your own dignity?

Answer #3: The right to abortion adds to every woman's dignity because it allows women to control their lives. No religion can be allowed to limit or dictate choice!

Question #4: Might you regret this abortion someday?

Answer #4: No. Women who have been able to obtain abortions maintain that it was the right decision. They have put a lot of thought into exercising their right.

Question #5: Can anything good be said about human abortion?

No Answer:

Question #6: Does good choice nurture life, or destroy life?

Answer #6: Good choice nurtures the lives of women.

Question #7: Why does the human fetus fight to stay alive?

Answer #7: A fetus is not a human being. It is dependent on a woman's life and cannot survive outside her womb.

Question #8: If feminism = human care, why destroy the unborn human?

Answer #8: Feminism = freedom from oppression and harassment. Help women exercise their right to accessible, legal abortion. Save women's lives.

Question #9: Is not all law based on a prior definition of human life?

No Answer:

Question #10: Can you imagine Jesus performing an abortion? Why not?

No Answer:

When I originally composed our signs, I had certain words underlined, words which were meant to quickly touch a point of response of the image of God in the readers. As well, the signs made no negative statements about or caricatures of any people, groups or political affiliations, but instead sought to get women to think in terms of their own dignity and power to make the right choice.

In reviewing this woman's selective responses, I had opportunity to reflect upon words which she had carefully chosen, and cared about deeply enough to commit to public language. And in her words, I see a reflection of the motivating pain behind the abortion-rights movement – the nature of male chauvinism.

In my first question, the focus was on you, getting women to think about their own humanity, their possession of life and gratefulness for it. With the R2N2 woman's response, I see aversion of the question. She did not say she was not glad to be alive (unaborted), but rather focused on her mother's dignity being preserved in resistance to being "forced." 2N2 woman must have been hurting enough to deflect the purpose of the question.

The R2N2 woman did not answer the second question. Perhaps she did not have time to prepare answers to all ten, and she chose the six she felt most interested in, or for which she was most able to give some answer. Or perhaps she, like many abortion-rights activists, was a woman who once had an abortion, one where she felt no choice as the father of the child refused any responsibility. Then in her pain at such chauvinistic treatment, she conflated an attempt to rationalize some dignity on her part by saying she had a choice to have an abortion, although her boyfriend actually gave her no choice. Maybe this was not the case with the R2N2 woman, but her answers indicate much pain, and such a scenario I have proposed has been true for too many other women.

(The new question #3 builds on question #2 with more specificity about the male influence, and hence his chauvinism.)

In her answer to (the original) question #3, the argument that "the right to abortion" adds dignity because "it allows women to control their lives," again seems to be a reaction against the chauvinistic treatment by men. And then her answer reflects an emphatic fear of impositional religion, which is a subject not even in view in this question. As well, all our signs, along with the banner, along with our non-blockade presence, equaled the opposite of limiting or dictating choice.

Even yet, though we try our best to succeed at the metaethics of language, some people have been violated too much by organized religion to see through their own pain to the substance of what we are trying to say. Our mere presence was interpreted viscerally on their part as a shoving of unwelcome religion down their throats. At times like this, gentleness in spirit, preceded by prayer, and augmented by eyeball to eyeball respect for her dignity as an image-bearer of God, is all the more important as we seek to hurdle these obstacles. As she relaxed a bit in my brief conversation with her, hopefully this was due to something of the goodness of the true Gospel touching her.

In the R2N2 woman's answer to question #4, the "no" answer seems defensive as much as it does personal. Most women do regret their abortions, modestly or completely, and the reality of post-abortion trauma is real and pervasive. And for many who say they do not regret it, a legitimate question is raised as to what extent a denial mechanism is in place to help salve the emotional pain. This woman may have had an abortion herself, and put much thought into it, though her sign put it in the third person. (And my experience leads me to view this as the likely scenario.) And having done so, no regrets are possible without an identity crisis such as the subconscious might suggest. And whereas she might have put much thought into it, many women being hurried off to an abortion appointment have not, and they are the ones that such a sign can reach at the last moment.

Question #5 went unanswered. Human abortion is an act of intrinsic destruction, and very hard to rationalize as "anything good." In the ten signs, the choice of what words were underlined sought an overall balance in focus, and this is the only one that actually focuses on the word abortion itself. In so doing, it focuses on the human nature of its object. It is all in an attempt to help focus on the humanity of the unborn child, which only in the touching of the mother's humanity, can we help to serve his or her rescue.

The answer to question #6 is again selective and defensive. It gives a true statement, but perhaps a false implication. Namely, the choice of human abortion does not serve womanhood's intrinsic nature, and only rarely is it necessary to actually save her life from an otherwise septic condition coincidental with pregnancy. If such rare cases were the sole focus of "abortion-rights," there would be no political turmoil. Good choice does not deliberately destroy human life.

In the answer to question #7, the denial of the unborn child's humanity is the only recourse. Interestingly, the Latin word fetus simply means "young one" in the personal and human sense. And yes, the fetus is dependent upon mom's womb, and indeed we are all dependent consistently upon the womb of the earth's ecosphere for daily survival. The R2N2 woman could have been asked, rhetorically in response, "And upon whom is a woman's life dependent? Her mother, father and the ecosphere, et al. and etc.? Who is not in some sense always dependent upon others?" And the R2N2 woman avoided the question of the fight. Namely, regardless of the semantics employed to dehumanize the unborn, we are all genetically programmed from our conceptions to be eager for life, to fight to live.

This eagerness is pre-conscious, and it energizes our self-awareness as it comes into full flower. The abortionist's scalpel must literally chase the unborn child inside his or her sanctuary in order to kill. The unborn child instinctively fights to stay alive, a point of identification which may help some abortion-minded women reconsider. But for the R2N2 woman, her pain of being hurt by religiously chauvinistic imposition may have been too great

73

for her to be willing to so identify with the unborn – even an unborn child as she was once herself.

The answer to question #8 is theologically most revealing. In the prior seven questions, I focused principally on the women coming in for an abortion appointment, seeking to empower them to choose life. Question #8 was aimed at the feminists present, asking them to consider the meaning of their own self-defining term of feminism. Feminist theory in its many permutations says specifically that if the world were run by women, and not by (chauvinistic) men, then we would have a more peaceful and ecologically friendly planet. Feminism is thus advertised as equaling "human care," and I sought in this question to link that assertion with caring for the unborn human. The R2N2 woman avoided this linkage and stated that feminism equals freedom from harassment. Amen – and only the power of informed choice can provide such freedom. But only because of the prior reality of Yahweh's power to give. Here the contrast between Genesis and all other sources for human identity is clear. The highest view of freedom outside of only Genesis is a negative freedom, a freedom from violation. But until violation is understood, freedom from it is not possible. Unless the order of creation, the reversal and the reversal of the reversal are understood, true freedom cannot be grasped.

Question #9 was designed as the one legal question, for any lawyers, government officials or even police officers who might take notice of it. As I describe my strategy for winning the legal protection of the unborn, the centrality of this question will be more fully understood. The question was phrased differently at the outset, changed slightly later, and she was reacting to the earlier phrasing.

Finally, question #10 addressed a theological concern, and the only one which I simultaneously answered, in this case with a rhetorical question.

74

Given the R2N2 woman's response to question #3 where she imported the question of religion, this might seem like a question that would have sparked a response on her part. The reason it did not, I suppose, is that it is one thing to castigate "religion" as an institution or force that oppresses people, and another thing to castigate Jesus as a person. In all of history, very few if any people have ever said anything negative about Jesus as a person, other than the religious and political elitists who opposed him when he was in the flesh – and as they did so knowingly without just cause. Even such elitists today are most hesitant to do so. His reputation is so singular, and also, who can honestly imagine the Son of God, who healed the lame and the blind, delivered the demonized and raised the dead – who could imagine him giving countenance to the surgical or chemical destruction of an unborn human child, on the ostensible grounds of the "right to choose"?

Once when I was holding this sign at Preterm, a woman abortion-rights supporter approached me and said how she resented me "forcing" religion on her. I asked her how I was doing this, and she pointed to my sign (original #10). I then asked how the sign "forced" religion on her, and she said that the mere introduction of the name of Jesus into such a political issue equaled such a "forcing."

She was receptive to dialogue, so I explained how the posing of the question was exactly that – a question. It required nothing of her and made no demands of her attention or action. It was one of ten questions we were posing, and the only one with explicit religious content. In fact, she was free not to read it or any of the other questions, and I was exercising my freedom of political expression in the use of such a sign, just as the abortion-rights supporters were doing with their own signs. She was at Preterm by her own volition, and no force was being applied to her to make her read the signs. As well, I noted that the question only has as much influence on people's thoughts and actions to the degree that they regard Jesus as someone whose person and teachings matter to them. If they believe Jesus is Lord and Savior, then the question raises a critical issue; if they regard Jesus as a mere human teacher, then the question raises concerns proportionate to how they view his teachings; if they do not give a whit about Jesus, then the question means nothing. I explained that many women coming in for an abortion have been raised with some sort of Christian teaching, and that my question might affect them positively as they intelligently reconsider their plans – that this equals the power of informed choice, the opposite of forcing religion on someone. For those abortion-minded women who do not care about what Jesus might think of abortion, the sign poses no force against their decision. Then I briefly profiled the nature of the power of informed choice, and her freedom to disregard the question if Jesus meant nothing to her.

Her response was lovely. She apologized for having misinterpreted the purpose of the sign, and thanked me for my explanation. I left it there. I did not probe about her opinion of Jesus Christ, nor was it appropriate at that juncture. The ethics of a biblical evangelism at this point is concerned with letting the Gospel be seen as Good News, and from there to trust the Holy Spirit to work in her heart and mind. She did not follow through with other questions, so I did not press her. But it was obvious that she thanked me for a gift given – an explanation for her gut level reaction to the question, and therefore I could see how her mind and emotions were happily catalyzed into considering what Jesus meant to her.

We also employed what is known as the Jeremiah 19 Liturgy, in which we also saw dramatic responses to this specific avenue of spiritual warfare.

The Jeremiah 19 Liturgy

Leader: We gather here today to seek the mercy of the one true Creator, to stop the killing of the unborn in this place. Hear the words of the prophet Jeremiah:

People: This is what Yahweh says: "Go and buy a clay jar from a potter. Take along some of the elders of the people and of the priests and go out to the Valley of Ben Hinnom, near the entrance of the Potsherd Gate. There proclaim the words I tell you."

Leader: The Valley of Ben Hinnom in 600 B.C. was used for places of Topheth, where infant children were burned alive to the Canaanite god Ba'al. Topheth means a fireplace for child sacrifice. Today we stand in front of an abortion center where human life is destroyed. It is a modern, updated Topheth shrine.

People: "Say, 'Hear the word of Yahweh, O kings of Judah and people of Jerusalem. This is what Yahweh Almighty, the God of Israel says: Listen! I am going to bring a disaster on this place that will make the ears of everyone who hears of it tingle.' "

Leader: Judah faced Yahweh's judgment in 586 B.C. with the destruction of Jerusalem and the temple they made into an idol, and thus the destruction of the nation, followed by their exile to Babylon. To the extent that this nation sanctions and continues the practice of human abortion, we invite Yahweh's judgment.

People: " 'For they have forsaken me and made this a place of foreign gods, they have burned sacrifices in it to gods that neither they nor their fathers nor the kings of Judah ever knew, and they have filled this place with the blood of the innocent." ' "

Leader: In the idolatry of Ba'al, the Hebrew people were seduced into believing that by burning their infant children alive they could gain fertility, peace and prosperity. Today we see an "idolatry of choice" where "choice" becomes a false god used to destroy unborn human life, instead of true choice which nurtures all human life.

In a life disrupted by a crisis pregnancy, human abortion is sold as a means to regain a lost sense of peace, order, stability and hope. But human abortion does not restore these shattered remains of God's image. Rather, it only fractures a broken life more deeply yet. This is idolatry, and we Christians are just as vulnerable to idolatry apart from God's grace.

People: " 'They have built the high places of Baal to burn their sons in the fire as offerings to Baal – something I did not command or mention, nor did it enter my mind. So beware, the days are coming, declares Yahweh, when people will no longer call this place Topheth or the Valley of Ben Hinnom, but the Valley of Slaughter.' "

Leader: This abortion center is a modern Topheth shrine, and a signpost to our own nation's judgment, to our own Valley of Slaughter. The victimizers become the victims, and one day human abortion will be remembered not as a woman's freedom or empowerment, but of her and her nation's slaughter. A slaughter not only of the unborn, but of women's dignity and men's dignity as life-nurturing humans.

People: " 'In this place I will ruin the plans of Judah and Jerusalem. I will make them fall by the sword before their enemies, at the hands of those who seek their lives, and I will give their carcasses as food to the birds of the air and the beasts of the earth. I will devastate this city and make it an object of scorn; all who pass by will be appalled and will scoff because of all its wounds. I will make them eat the flesh of their sons and daughters, and they will eat one another's flesh during the stress of the siege imposed upon them by the enemies who seek their lives.' "

Leader: Jerusalem's idolatrous sacrifice of her infant children led to a literal cannibalism. This nation's destruction of her unborn progeny cries out for a modern equivalent. Family fratricide, social disintegration, drug abuse, sexual abuse, homosexual glorification, violent crime and coercive euthanasia equal the "writing on the wall."

The harvesting and cloning of human embryos for research and transplants is its own form of human cannibalism. And why do we presume that we are above the descent into literal cannibalism one day? From the ground beneath our feet there cries out the blood of millions of unborn U.S. citizens. We will reap what we have sown, apart from God's mercy which triumphs over judgment for those who seek him.

People: "Then break the jar while those who go with you are watching, and say to them, 'This is what Yahweh Almighty says: I will smash this nation and this city just as this potter's jar is smashed and cannot be repaired.' "

Leader: The jar Jeremiah used was similar to that used to bury the charred remains of the sacrificed children. And the parents truly wept as they buried them. This is the terror of idolatry. But today, the idolatry of human abortion hides the terrible act of its destruction within the machinery of the suction apparatus, or through the assault of toxic chemicals. There are no coffins, no tombstones, and too often the grief remains hidden and festering.

As surely as Jeremiah's breaking of the symbolic clay jar signaled Yahweh's impending judgment, we believe Yahweh Elohim pronounces judgment upon the sites and apparatus of human abortion, and upon those who cling to its idolatry while mocking the Lord and Giver of life. As Jerusalem became like Topheth, so too will the ethos of human abortion kill the culture that enshrines it.

Therefore I break this jar as a prayer for Yahweh Elohim to bring an end to the evil of human abortion, and the male chauvinisms that undergird it. We thus proclaim Yahweh's love to the women and their unborn children so victimized. I also break this jar as a symbol to break the powers of darkness which govern the abortion mind-set. In the name of Jesus Messiah, Yahweh Elohim incarnate, let it be.

[break jar]

People: " 'They will bury the dead in Topheth until there is no more room. This is what I will do to this place and to those who live here, declares Yahweh. I will make this city like Topheth. The houses in Jerusalem and those of the kings of Judah will be defiled in this place, Topheth – all the houses where they burned incense on the roofs to all the starry hosts and poured out drink offerings to other gods.' "

Leader: When Jeremiah broke the clay jar, he declared that he was not the Judge. He trusted Yahweh Elohim as the only righteous Judge, and faithfully called upon King Zedekiah and the other leaders to put an end to the shedding of innocent blood. To do so, they had to first put away the sins of sorcery and worshiping the stars, which leads to human sacrifice.

Likewise we trust in the one true Creator and the power of loving persuasion in the public arena. No people are our enemies, even those who perform or support human abortion. Only the devil and his demonic host are our enemies. Thus we seek to win hearts and minds through the truth, love and beauty of the Gospel of Jesus Messiah. We seek the fullest dignity for women and their unborn children equally.

People: Thus we affirm:

- Yes to the marriage of one man and one woman for one lifetime.
- Yes to loving and faithful fatherhood.
- Yes to women and their unborn.
- Yes to the image of God in all people – born and unborn.
- Yes to the power to give in face of the power to take.
- Yes to informed choice which serves human life.
- Yes to the power to bless in the face of the power to curse.
- Yes to the power of love in face of the power to hate.
- Yes to the Good News of Jesus the Messiah.

People: Jeremiah then returned from Topheth, where Yahweh had sent him to prophesy, and stood in the court Yahweh's temple and said to all the people, "This is what Yahweh Almighty, the God of Israel, says: 'Listen! I am going to bring on this city and the villages around it every disaster I pronounced against them, because they were stiff-necked and would not listen to my words.' "

Leader: We are all stiff-necked apart from God's grace, and we who are believers welcome the toughest questions from abortion supporters who might be seeking the same grace in the midst of their broken lives.

People: Jeremiah also says, "See, I am setting before you the way of life and the way of death." And Moses says, "Now choose life." So listen to the words of Jeremiah spoken to King Zedekiah, "This is what Yahweh says: Do what is just and right. Rescue from the hand of his oppressor the one who has been robbed. Do no wrong or violence to the alien, the fatherless or the widow, and do not shed innocent blood."

Leader: Jeremiah promised peace for Israel if King Zedekiah were to obey. The same promise is before us today, if we as a nation, beginning with our leaders, would turn away from the slaughter of unborn human children.

If there is no true Creator in heaven who judges the acts of men and women, and if Jesus Messiah is not who he said he was, then abortion supporters can be at ease. For if this is the case, all we do is break a piece of pottery in an act of feebleness.

But if the one true Creator is the one true Creator, then this symbol of the broken jar is inescapable. The idolatry of human abortion is in direct opposition to the Creator and Author of human life. And we will all stand at the judgment seat of our heavenly Father one day.

Forgiveness is offered to all who seek it, and it is complete in its healing of past sorrow and guilt for those who dare to believe.

People: We say to all who would listen:

- You have the power to choose life, if you dare to believe it and ask God for it.
- If you do not have this power, what power and choice do you have?
- If you have power and choice, why not use it?
- Courageous and compelling choice always nurtures human life, and in Jesus Messiah, such courage, power and choice is uniquely available.

Amen.

◆ ◆ ◆

Chapter Five

The Ministers Affirmation on Marriage and "The Pain That Dares Not Speak Its Name"

An Eight-Fold Agenda

In 1994, I wrote a diagnosis of the homosexual-rights movement, summing up an eight-fold agenda which I then discerned, and have tweaked it only slightly in the meantime. It is the relentless agenda of a small core of homosexual-rights activists that will outlast the core of politically defined pro-family activists, unless biblical theology gains ascendancy. Most homosexual persons are not pressing for this agenda – they are oftentimes hurting persons, needing the love of Christ, or persons who want merely to be left alone. But there is a small core, even a core within a shifting core, which consists of those who press the agenda with the help of a willing culture within syncretistic churches, politics, academia and the education establishment, the media, business, professional disciplines and the arts. Here is the agenda:

1. Remove the concept of homosexuality as "sinful," and remove the concept that homosexual behavior is intrinsically unhealthy.

2. Define homosexual identity and behavior as a "normal" and healthy "variant" within the plurality of the human community, and call for "toleration" of it.

3. Move from "toleration" of it as a "normal variant," to a full "acceptance" of its intrinsic nature as being equal with that of heterosexuality.

4. Gain ecclesiastical, legal and social "approval" of the personal and social "goodness" of homosexuality, and call it "gay."
5. Translate this "approval" into leadership positions – especially ordination status in the church and political office in the culture.
6. Redefine "marriage" to include "same-sex" relationships.
7. Elevate "gay" relationships to a place of moral superiority for the wider culture to honor and emulate.
8. Define "homophobia," "hate speech" and/or "hate crimes" as the cardinal theological and political "sins," and remove the First Amendment liberties of anyone who disagrees, including those of ministers, rabbis and priests who refuse to perform same-sex marriage ceremonies; and at the extreme, remove the protection of unalienable rights for dissenters to this "new orthodoxy."

Agenda items #1 through #5 are already deeply infused within the culture, and items #6 through #8 continue to be aggressively pursued. As I examine elsewhere, the 2004 *Goodridge* decision of the Massachusetts Supreme Judicial Court forced same-sex marriage on the Commonwealth in deep violation of the State Constitution; followed by cognate rulings. Namely, they elevated same-sex marriage to the status of a "fundamental" or "basic civil right," indeed, equal to that of an unalienable right. This reality almost never gains comment, but is the deepest substance of the decision, and its greatest threat to civil life. For if same-sex marriage is an unalienable right, what happens to the historically preceding reality of religious liberty as an unalienable right? And religious liberty is the first freedom from which the freedoms of speech, press, assembly and redress of grievances follow. This conflict percolates in an ever-widening capacity when it comes to the eight-fold agenda.

In response to this agenda, in specific concern, an ad hoc group of ministers in Connecticut asked me to write a Ministers Affirmation on Marriage, which twice we published in the Hartford Courant – it proved above reproach. But before we look at it, we need to know the realities that are far deeper, and where the human soul needs ministry. Thus, here are five vignettes from ministry.

The Surprising Testimony of Three Lesbians at Harvard

In my Th.M. studies at Harvard in the 1980s, I was taking a class in feminist ethics, and as a white male heterosexual evangelical pro-life minister, I was an exception.

One day during lunch, about two weeks into the term, three women classmates approached me as I was sitting in the refectory. One of them introduced herself and her two friends as they pulled up chairs, and she said, "You know John, for an evangelical, you're a nice guy."

An oxymoron?

She continued, and introduced a topic de novo. She noted that the three of them were lesbian, and that every lesbian they knew had been the victim of "physical, sexual and/or emotional abuse" by some man in her early years.

This was new information to me. And why, I still wonder, were they sharing it with me?

These women were in the middle of a large and international nexus of lesbians in the university rich Boston area, and thus this anecdote carried great power (though not being a statistical claim).

In only a minority of instances is the biological father implicated in the abuse. Rather it is a stepfather, live-in boyfriend of the mother, some extended family member, or some other man with access to the household who is the usual perpetrator (apart from those who are violated by other teenagers, or adults, as teenagers).

In other words, the abuse is usually the result of the chosen or de facto absence of the biological father – the absence of the one who is supposed to love, cherish and protect them in the unique power to give of godly fatherhood.

I remember praying in my spirit as I heard these words, *Dear God above, has the church ever heard this? Or do we merely pass judgment on those who are homosexual and move on?*

I thought to myself, *These are women for whom Christ died, to offer them the gift of eternal life. How well are we in the church communicating such good news?*

When Jesus encountered the woman at the well, and the woman caught in the act of adultery (probably a set-up), how did he approach them? How well do we hear the heart cries of those who suffer, and thus, in the extreme, try to reshape society to shield themselves against any further suffering? Until we address this reality, we, the church, will be easily shouted down in an increasingly lawless society.

The Pain That Dares Not Speak Its Name

If first we win honest relationships in the face of tough questions, the debates are far easier to address. With such a focus, the Gospel takes center stage in its power to redeem politics, culture, the nation, indeed, all the nations.

In 1895, Oscar Wilde spoke of "the love that dares not speak its name" in his public trial for homosexual conduct. Even now, with homosexual identity openly proclaiming its name – along with a growing wave of legal endorsements – there remains the prior gnawing tumor of "the pain that dares not speak its name."

This reality is the most closely guarded injury to the human soul. So long as it remains hidden and festering, those who suffer only suffer more, and those who shape public policy to cover this soul pain only multiply the suffering further.

In 2002 I spoke of this pain to a crowded assembly in the Connecticut State Legislature. The main hearing room was packed with 200 people before the Judiciary Committee, and two overflow rooms of 200 each were linked by close-circuit television, and broadcast live on CT-N.

The overwhelming majority of the same-sex marriage advocates were women, wearing yellow stickers identifying their advocacy. They were there early, accounting for perhaps 120 of those in the main room, whereas the clear majority for all three hearing rooms together believed otherwise.

I was on a panel of those testifying in favor of marriage as one man and one woman. Our time was limited greatly by a political enterprise that had a foregone conclusion already in place.

I set the stage with the story from my studies at Harvard. And when I mentioned "Harvard," there was a wave of gasps across the room, as if to say, "Surely no one who has gone to Harvard could possibly say no to same-sex marriage." The name "Harvard" does carry cachet, but I am not impressed. I enjoyed ninth grade so much, I took it twice ("third form" in the English prep school system into which my father wisely transferred me – I actually had to learn to do homework).

Then I gave the testimony of my three fellow students – professing lesbians who spoke of the reality that all other lesbians they knew had suffered physical, sexual and/or emotional abuse as young girls.

As I mentioned this abuse to the legislative assembly, I could hardly hear myself speak as a cacophony of spontaneous groans filled the room. Afterward, a friend told me that all the groans came from women wearing the same-sex marriage stickers. Accordingly, they literally held their breaths until I was done with this thought.

I thus realized I had spoken a publicly unspoken pain, while seeking to affirm the human dignity of those who know such suffering; but also being unprepared for the searing depths of emotion that were unleashed.

It was a pain that I, as an evangelical minister, was not supposed to know about, much less, care about. In other words, I do live as much of my life as possible among various skeptics of the Gospel (or in truth, among skeptics of the church who do not yet grasp the Gospel). Jesus always sought out the disenfranchised and hurting.

Despite this response to my testimony, the media had no interest in follow through, and never even attempted to criticize it. Silence. This is a forbidden question in politics and media, for such abuse, and any range of hurts, is far broader than that known in the homosexual world. Abuse cuts through the lives of so many people from so many angles.

As a minister of the Gospel, I have deep anguish for the pain that dares not name itself, for the undeserved shame and suffering imposed on so many children and teenagers. Jesus says: "Come to me, all you who are weary, and I will give you rest" (Matthew 11:28).

How well do we in the church communicate the Gospel in the face of the pain and acrimony of this political debate? Do those who struggle with homosexual temptation see in us the Good News, or merely a competing political idolatry of winning the debate at all costs?

Winning an Honest Friendship with a Most Effective Lesbian Activist

In November, 2002 I addressed a Mars Hill Forum at Boston University with Arline Isaacson: "Is Same-Sex Marriage Good for the Nation?"

Arline is co-chair of the Massachusetts Gay and Lesbian Political Caucus, and perhaps the most strategically effective lesbian activist in the nation. She organized fellow activists in 1989 to lobby the legislature for the first in the nation "Gay Rights Bill," and in 2004, Arline led the lobbying effort for the legislature to yield to a court-imposed same-sex marriage bill, again, first in the nation.

That evening I arrived first, as students were filing into the lecture hall. Of the 220 or so people there, maybe 40-50 were known to be Christian and on my side of the question. When Arline arrived – the first time I had ever met her – I reached out with a smile, shook her hand, and said, "A pleasure to meet you."

Arline had a coterie of homosexual activists following her into the room, and as I said these words, they all literally fell back 1-2 feet. The shock was deeply apparent. I was supposed to be a "homophobe" and not a gracious person toward Arline or them.

Arline gave the opening address, answering yes to the question. In her first words, even as I call this a forum, and not a debate, she said, "In debating John Rankin tonight on this issue, it is the first time I am not debating someone who palpably hates me." I was blown away – especially if indeed she has debated others who have conveyed hatred for her person.

Later in the evening, during the question and answer period, Arline looked at me and said, "John – we know that you love us." Yet I never used the word "love." Rather I showed her unfailing respect as an image-bearer of God even as I fully disagreed with her about same-sex marriage.

Our second forum was at Harvard in March, 2004, just weeks before the Massachusetts legislature voted on the same-sex marriage bill. Several times Arline asked me, in different words, "John, why are you trying to harm me and my family by opposing same-sex marriage?" I was incredulous, and the audience was energized at this question. Arline has two biological children by artificial insemination, raising them with her partner.

So finally I gave response along these lines: "Arline – the real harm has been done by the male chauvinists who sold their sperm for fifty bucks and don't give a damn about their children." And her children were conceived years before same-sex marriage was a possibility. Quiet. These are the most caustic words I have spoken in any forum.

Yet Arline was eager for another forum, which came to pass in October, 2008, at the largest church in New England. At the end she gave me a hug, knowing well that we disagree completely on the subject. In other words, if we first win an honest friendship, tough and true words can be spoken if the moment requires it.

Sometime later, Arline emailed me, and has given me permission to quote her: "John, you are a true gentleman and a thoughtful advocate." Is this what we expect from a most effective lesbian activist? If not, then perhaps we do not understand the yearning humanity deep inside all persons, except those few who have died to such humanity while continuing to breathe the air for a season.

Now, in the raging debate over same-sex marriage, do we invest in the power to show love as we pursue truth? As did Jesus? Or will be become entrapped in the broken egos of political debate as an end in itself? I have also developed many other honest friendships with various leading homosexual advocates.

Empty Intimidation by a Same-Sex Marriage Attorney at Smith College

In February, 2004, I addressed a Mars Hill Forum on same-sex marriage at Smith College, in Northampton, Massachusetts. The state's Supreme Judicial Court (SJC) had just made a ruling essentially forcing the legislature to pass a bill legalizing same-sex marriage.

It was a feisty event with the audience, and in particular, with an attorney after the forum..

One Christian student sat among some twenty fellow students prior to the forum's start, all avowed lesbians. They were saying how I was going to be chewed up and made ready for shark bait, and they were ready for it. After all, I was a white heterosexual male, an evangelical pro-life minister – six strikes against me before I stood up. But as the forum progressed, they started to complain, "He's being too gracious…"

I made three observations to start the evening. First, I told the audience that I wanted them all to succeed in attaining the fruit of being image-bearers of God – peace, order, stability and hope, to live, to love, to laugh and to learn. The question is how we best achieve these goals, whether on God's terms, or on our own broken terms.

Second, I stated that I did not want one inch of greater liberty to speak what I believe, than the liberty I first commend to those who disagree with me. The Golden Rule in political context. And third, if any homosexual person there happened to be facing danger, and if I were in position to intervene to protect his or her life, I would do so instinctively.

After the forum, an attorney approached me and introduced himself. He had clerked for the SJC in its *Goodridge* decision legalizing same-sex marriage. He asked if I had read the decision and I said yes. He then called me a liar several times. So I started quoting it extensively on the spot, and he changed the subject after admitting I understood it.

He had wanted to intimidate me into silence. After all, who was I as a minister to address legal matters? He needed to prove me out of my league and unqualified. This attempt grew comical yet tragic. He emailed me several times afterward, having looked at my website. He was concerned with a "disturbing pattern" of me going from campus to campus "stirring up ideological antagonism toward the indigenous gay students ..." and what I am doing is "very, very hateful and arrogant" and "meddlesome."

He recommended that I change my occupation, diagnosed my emotional insecurity of "clinging desperately" to the Bible, and finally my need to go on a 30-day (pagan) "Insight Meditation" retreat, where I would learn to "SHUT UP AND LISTEN for a change ..."

Imagine that. A biblical opinion on same-sex marriage is so rarely heard on pagan and secular campuses, and there I was at Smith College, the most pro-lesbian college in the nation, in Northampton, Massachusetts with its reputation for the heaviest concentration of serious witchcraft. No matter my articulation of the image of God, freedom of speech and willingness to risk my life for a homosexual person – I was being told to shut up.

While this man was speaking with me, a young woman interrupted him, graciously and with great poise. She said to me, "Thank you for coming. I am struggling. Can we talk sometime?" She had been an atheist, daughter of a physicist, came to Christ within two weeks time, began to deal with some deep pain in her life, and then to grow wonderfully in the Lord.

Also, following the forum, the prime sponsor, the Smith Christian Fellowship, grew remarkably in size. Many lesbians approached them afterward and thanked them for sponsoring an event where both sides were heard.

In addressing the debate over same-sex marriage, there are twin dangers for the church. A core of homosexual activists would like to a) goad us into hateful speech, or b) intimidate us into silence.

But if we truly love our neighbors as ourselves, as God has loved us, then we will fall prey to neither. Then we have authority to show how same-sex marriage is not good for anyone, and as it only deepens human pain while tearing apart the social order.

A Smart Lesbian Attorney Aiming for a U.S. Supreme Court Ruling: Has the Church a Clue?

Same-sex marriage headed for the U.S. Supreme Court, and does the church have even the slightest clue on how to address the question?

Attorney Mary L. Bonauto won the *Goodridge* case before the Massachusetts Supreme Judicial Court (SJC) in 2003, where the Court ordered the legislature to pass a same-sex marriage law. And at the time, Governor Mitt Romney had the constitutional authority to hold the SJC accountable for its extra-legal interference with the legislature. But he did not do so. Mary is also the lead attorney arguing against the federal Defense of Marriage Act (DOMA).

I met Mary at the University of Connecticut (UConn) School of Law in March, 2012, and spoke with her afterward, and have been in touch by email several times since.

Mary is a patient strategic thinker, key to the same-sex marriage movement, articulate and gracious in demeanor. Her legal goal for 22 years has been the enshrinement of same-sex marriage as a fundamental constitutional right, and she has come a long way in that pursuit.

When I heard Mary speak at UConn, it was attended by a modest audience, mostly lawyers. They were on her side of the issue. And even as she spoke to a friendly group, she never once demonized or spoke disparagingly of any person who opposes her position.

Yet too, she also stated that in all her years of interacting with people who oppose same-sex marriage – or "marriage equality" as she calls it – they were people with a visceral disgust of homosexuality and its practices. In other words, she felt treated as sub-human. She did not believe their arguments had anything to do with constitutional law.

This is not how Jesus treats people. His loves draws them into the light – it does not drive them into deeper darkness. Those who wind up in the darkness do so out of their chosen resistance to Jesus, as he made clear in his conversation with Nicodemus.

In her presentation, Mary was accurate in telling the history of the legal battle over same-sex marriage. But she was also very shrewd in what she did not say. There are two major issues upon which same-sex marriage will either rise or fall when it reaches the U.S. Supreme Court. Mary did not raise the first issue – the Source for unalienable rights, upon which all civil rights are by definition predicated. And with the second one – the mnatter of of "immutable traits" – she made a remarkable grammatical construct that admitted it, but while deftly redefining it at the same time.

I have read the *Goodridge* (Massachusetts), *Re: Marriage Cases* (California) and *Kerrigan* (Connecticut) decisions in detail. These are the first three court rulings in favor of same-sex marriage that set the template for all else that has followed. In these rulings, these two central issues have not been honestly addressed. Nor since. And thus, the need for the Minister's Affirmation on Marriage before the U.S. Supreme Court. I know of no other way to present the proper argument in the right spirit.

———————————

The Ministers Affirmation on Marriage

www.ministersaffirmation.org

In the politics of debate, and in various Court rulings and State Legislatures, same-sex marriage has been advanced:

1. Apart from the historical nature of unalienable and constitutional rights;

2. Often in direct threat to the religious, political and economic liberty of dissenters, and;

3. Without making the case for defining homosexuality as an objective civil rights class.

These three realities ultimately undermine a civil society for all people. Rooted in the initial Ministers Affirmation on Marriage published in the Hartford Courant in 2003 and 2005, this Affirmation has been presented many times to the most qualified and committed advocates of same-sex marriage, and continues to seek their input. Now, in preparation for a likely U.S. Supreme Court case, this Affirmation is set to be presented as an *amicus* ("friend of the court" legal brief), with full annotation, and seeking as many signatories as possible.

- To be a signatory, in agreeing to this Affirmation, email tei@teii.org with your full contact information, and position in ministry or teaching. And please, do whatever study is necessary to understand what is both a simple, yet biblically and constitutionally literate affirmation. All clergy recognized by their local churches and/or larger denominations, and other recognized leaders such as elders, deacons, pastoral staff, Sunday School and Bible Study leaders, Christian school or university educators, missionaries, leaders in

Christian organizations, Christians who are educators in secular settings, et al., qualify. In other words, Christian leaders who are actively involved in shaping the church and its pedagogy in the face of the wider culture.

An Affirmation by Ministers of the Gospel and Christian Leaders:

Yes to Man and Woman in Marriage
No to Same-Sex Marriage

First, we affirm that the unalienable rights of life, liberty and property, and hence the power to pursue happiness, are given by the Creator to all people equally, as individual people, regardless of religion, sexual identity or other criteria. This affirmation is rooted uniquely in the assumptions and trajectory of Genesis 1-2, and reflected in the Declaration of Independence and the U.S. Constitution.

We also affirm that the Creator defines human sexuality in the context of the marriage of one man and one woman in mutual fidelity. Here, the equality and complementary of male and female serves diversity in service to unity, uniquely providing the necessary social adhesive of trust, which is then modeled for our children.

In human history, no society rooted in the approval of homosexuality, in any capacity, has ever produced unalienable rights for the larger social order.

Nonetheless, same-sex marriage has been advanced, without historical precedent, as a de facto unalienable right ("basic" or "fundamental"). Therefore, we believe same-sex marriage advocates need to answer four questions:

1. Are unalienable rights being redefined?

2. If so, why?

3. If so, what is the new basis for these rights?

4. If so, what are the consequences? For example, would the "right" to same-sex marriage thus prevail over the religious, political and economic liberty to dissent from it? And, can a descent into "might make right" thus be averted?

Second, "sexual orientation" is changeable, even if deeply present in one's psyche, and there is no scientific basis for a supposed genetic or social determinism to homosexuality. Therefore, we believe same-sex marriage advocates need to answer two further questions:

1. What is the evidence that homosexuality is a fixed and "immutable trait," and thus equal to an objective class of people for separate civil rights purposes?

2. What prevents any other group of people from claiming a subjective identity as a civil rights class?

Unless these six questions are answered with clarity and substance, then same-sex marriage advocates have not sustained their position.

And finally, we affirm these words of Jesus: "Come to me, all you who are weary, and I will give you rest" (Matthew 11:28).

For those who struggle with homosexual temptation, or any other temptation, Jesus invites us to come to him, and on his terms. We too, as ministers of the Gospel, and leaders in the church, have the exact same need, daily, to seek God's grace to overcome any range of temptations that may come our way – as is common with all people.

Jesus affirms marriage as defined in the biblical order of creation, he fulfilled the Law of Moses that says no to homosexual actions, and the apostle Paul ratifies the same. Therefore, those who wish to be reconciled with the biblical understanding of Jesus are invited to affirm marriage as one man and one woman, and to eschew all other definitions of human sexuality.

All people are created as image-bearers of God, seeking peace, order, stability and hope; to live, to love, to laugh and to learn. The question is whether we seek these qualities on our Creator's own terms, or on our own broken terms. And we are all broken, in one way or another, apart from the healing power of the Gospel.

It is one thing to address the political world with solid ideas, yet in truth there is very little substantive thinking in American political life today, at least at the level of office holders and seekers. In the Ministers Affirmation on Marriage, it moves from ideas to concrete emotional realities when it addresses the matter needing rest for the soul, and in the struggle with temptation. Below is a bold, risky and true statement is set forth that is new with the publication of this edition. It aims at the leverage needed for the human heart to consider political ideas that are actually honest and in service to a full and shared humanity. Here, it is profoundly "first the Gospel, then politics ..."

♦ ♦ ♦

see also:

www.sevenquestions.org

Chapter Six

Changing the Metaphor for Church and State

On April 11, 2007 I addressed a Mars Hill Forum at Patrick Henry College with Barry Lynn, executive director of Americans United for Separation of Church and State, looking at this issue. Barry responded well to my argument, though not agreeing that the metaphor of "the wall of separation between church and state" needs to be changed. We found no stated disagreements in terms of history or biblical ethics – it was more a matter of a different political prism he holds, where we both say no to state-established religion (but beyond that have great disagreements on theology, issues and policies). I argued that "the wall of separation" is a negative metaphor, and only divides; my proposal is for the positive metaphor of "a level playing field" for all religious and political ideas. Here is my prepared text for the evening (with some slight edits).

Good evening in the name of Jesus, the incarnate God of the Bible, Yahweh Elohim. This greeting is appropriate for me to give in any setting where people yearn for religious, political and economic liberty – for these liberties are part of the unalienable rights upon that this nation is founded. Historically, unalienable rights have only one Source – the God of the Bible, and they are given in the biblical order of creation. And I desire and pray for all people to enjoy these liberties equally. Of necessity, we need this foundation to address our question tonight: "What is the Nature of the Separation between Church and State?"

To wit: the nature is rooted in the simple metaphor of a wall, and metaphors can be wonderfully instructive, and as easily misleading. Dr. Daniel Dreisbach of American University, in his definitive work, *Thomas Jefferson and the Wall of Separation between Church and State*, focuses on the nature of the metaphor as Jefferson and others used it.

Tonight I will seek to define the use of this metaphor, and why I consider it a poor one to begin with, even before it was later misused. It is both reactive and negative in nature. Then I will propose a new metaphor, which is proactive and positive in nature. It is also quintessentially radical, being rooted in the biblical order of creation and the person of Jesus.

I am particularly interested to see what my colleague Barry Lynn thinks of my metaphor, for indeed, his organization, Americans United for Separation of Church and State, roots its identity in its interpretation of the metaphor, "a wall of separation."

On January 1, 1802, President Thomas Jefferson answered a letter from the Danbury Baptist Association of Connecticut. The Baptists were grateful for his election in the bitterly contested 1800 campaign against President John Adams. They highly regarded Jefferson's well-known views on religious liberty.

Adams was vociferously supported by the New England Congregationalist clergy establishment, which was in lockstep with political Federalism, and they called Jefferson an infidel and atheist. The Congregationalists came from the Puritans and had some excellent original theology, especially in terms of the concept of vocation or "calling," and the economic power it unleashed still blesses this nation. But it also had a central weakness, seeking to establish an earthly theocracy, where all citizens in Massachusetts and Connecticut in the 17th century either had to be Congregationalist, or by the force of state taxes, they had to support the Congregational Church.

Later, non-Congregationalists were exempted from these taxes, so long as they verifiably attended some other Christian church. But the Baptists complained that this was only a human privilege of "toleration" being given by the establishment – truly a condescending negative. They rightly wanted equal access to the unalienable right of religious liberty – a true positive for all people.

In his letter of response to the Danbury Baptists, Jefferson saw that it was published widely and immediately, taking advantage of the opportunity to strike back at the Congregationalist clergy and the Federalist political establishment, a) to rebut the charge he was an infidel and atheist, and b) to advance the cause of Republicanism – that is, the preeminence of state's rights in view of a limited federal government. He used language that kept the federal government out of institutional religion, lauded freedom of conscience in religious matters, and then used the famous metaphor: "I contemplate with sovereign reverence that act of the whole American people which declared that *their* legislature should 'make no law respecting an establishment of religion, or prohibiting the free exercise thereof,' thus building a wall of separation between Church & State ..." The letter was not wholly satisfactory to the Danbury Baptists, but largely so, even as Jefferson used it for his own purposes.

Jefferson was quoting the First Amendment before using the metaphor, yet he was in France at the time of its composition and ratification from 1787 through 1791. Thus his metaphor is neither constitutional nor should it be legally definitive. And, unlike much modern interpretive gloss, it does not separate political and religious life.

As the exegesis of Dr. Dreisbach sustains, Jefferson referred to a wall of separation between the federal government on the one hand, and state government and the institutional church on the other. It was not a wall separating religious life and political life. Though he rightly opposed an established Anglican church in his native Virginia, nonetheless as Governor he signed "A Proclamation Appointing a Day of Publick and Solemn Thanksgiving and Prayer" in November, 1779. He opposed the federal government doing the same, and thus was charged by Adams and the Federalists of being an infidel and atheist. In other words, he was acting as a partisan Republican against partisan Federalists. The texture of reality is not so facile as it might otherwise appear.

Now I say he rightly opposed a state established church, based on principles of religious liberty. But even yet, as President he did not seek to have the Congress require the same of Massachusetts and Connecticut, both of which still had state establishment of the Congregational Church. He believed it was a state issue to resolve, not a federal one, and as it turned out, it was resolved within two decades. The Danbury Baptists wanted disestablishment, not the language of a wall of separation, and even though Jefferson agreed in principal, he was not a Federalist, and did not appease them here by interfering with state politics.

Jefferson's wall was not regarded as anything definitive by his peers, and largely fell out of the public eye, apart from a fleeting appearance in 1879. But in 1947, in the *Everson v. Board of Education* U.S. Supreme Court Decision, Justice Hugo Black quoted the metaphor and added something novel to it. It was something both non-Jeffersonian and non-constitutional, saying such a wall should be "high and impregnable." Americans United for Separation of Church and State was founded the same year, and ever since, the wall metaphor has been used by them and the American Civil Liberties Union (ACLU) et al. to separate much government and religion in a sense that is foreign to Jefferson's purpose. As some scholars say, it is the wall that Hugo Black built.

But at the prior level, how does the wall metaphor actually apply to the substance of the First Amendment itself?

The First Amendment reads: "Congress shall make no law respecting an establishment of religion, or prohibiting the free exercise thereof; or abridging the freedom of speech, or of the press, or of the right of the people peaceably to assemble, and to petition the Government for a redress of grievances."

Against a backdrop of nationally established churches in Europe, the Anglican Church in England, the Roman Catholic Church in France and the Lutheran Church in Germany, for example, the seeds of religious liberty grew well in the Colonies and nascent United States. In the one and a half centuries from the Puritans in Plymouth, and through the power of the First Great Awakening, the finest fruit of the Reformation began to take hold by the time of the Declaration of Independence in 1776 and the First Amendment in 1787 – no political coercion in religion. Laws only apply to actions, even as Jefferson stated in his Danbury letter just prior to what I quoted earlier: "religion is a matter which lies solely between Man & his God, that he owes account to none other for his faith or his worship, that the legitimate powers of government reach actions only, & not opinions ..."

Critically here, the First Amendment is a restriction on the federal government, and for the sake of protecting the four liberties that follow. There is no restriction on religion, even as established by a state (and if a person did not like one state's established religion, he or she could freely move to another state). The federal government shall make no laws setting up an established institutional church, which would be discriminatory, and this is what "establishment of religion" means. On such a basis, it shall not prohibit the freedom of religion, whether in the individual conscience or the freedom of people to form an institutional church. The federal government shall have no veto powers over the church, and since no institutional church is established by the United States, none has a privileged position to make demands of the federal government. This is a type of natural distinction, but not for the sake of a "high and impregnable" wall of opposing camps with the federal government as master; but for the sake of a mutual cooperation in the pursuit of religious, political and economic liberties.

What this means is that all people are equally free to participate in political life, based explicitly on what they believe, whether as Jews, Christians, Muslims, Hindus, Buddhists, pagans, atheists or otherwise – so long as we all honor the equal access to political life and argument for those who believe otherwise, all within the rule of law.

Too, if Hugo Black's "high and impregnable wall" were literally in view in the First Amendment text, then as the syntax would then make clear, any range of particular religious expression can be banned or severely limited in government. Thus likewise, speech, the press, public assembly and redress of the government can also be banned or severely limited. The First Amendment is clear – religious liberty is the first freedom; and only when we are free to believe what we choose, do we then have the freedom to speak those beliefs, publish those beliefs, assemble on the basis of those beliefs, and critically, to redress and challenge government policies based on those beliefs.

Earlier I said that the metaphor of "a wall of separation" is reactive and negative. Any wall that isolates is by definition negative. But history also shows why negatives happen – this is the nature of war, even a just war waged to protect the innocent. But ultimately, if we only react to the reactions or negatives of others, we will all drown in the same miserable soup. Hugo Black's "high and impregnable" wall of separation was crafted against a long historical backdrop of religious intolerance, and hopefully none of us here want such intolerance.

So, how and where can the proactive and positive gain the greater influence?

Here the language of Jefferson is helpful – as the scribe for the Committee that drafted the Declaration of Independence, even as the heterodox rationalist he was.

In the Declaration, we read these words: "WE hold these Truths to be self-evident, that all Men are created equal, that they are endowed by their Creator with certain unalienable Rights, that among these are Life, Liberty, and the Pursuit of Happiness – That to secure these Rights, Governments are instituted among Men, deriving their just Powers from the Consent of the Governed ..."

By definition, "unalienable rights" are those rights that human government cannot define, give or take away. They can only be acknowledged as prior to and greater than the existence of human government, and which human government must serve. Jefferson and his colleagues knew that by appealing to the Creator, that King George III could not trump them in any way – for though he was violating the lives, liberties and property rights of the Colonists, and could lay claim as the highest human authority for the British Colonies, even as the humanly defined head of the Anglican Church, he could not trump the God of the Bible. Thus, Jefferson the rationalist, Franklin the deist becoming a theist, Paine the "freethinker" and the other 53 signatories – the vast majority of whom were actively or formally orthodox Protestants, with one bold Roman Catholic in their midst – they all agreed on a theological and historical point of reference.

No pagan religion or secular construct has ever conceived of such unalienable rights. In pagan religions, the gods and goddesses beat up on

104

each other and on us – the very opposite of unalienable rights. In the Epicurean swerve that presaged Darwinian macroevolution, the universe does not know we exist, spits us forth and swallows us up with no concept of unalienable rights. The deism of the Enlightenment is likewise impotent – being a philosophical idea of an amorphous and ahistorical deity that has no articulation or concept of unalienable rights.

The unalienable rights were expressed in the Declaration with a Jeffersonian philosophical flair – "life, liberty and the pursuit of happiness." In the Fifth and Fourteen Amendments, they are legally more precise in the third instant, "life, liberty and property." The liberties in view are codified in the First Amendment – religion, speech, the press, assembly and redress of grievances; and summarily covered in the arenas of religious, political and economic liberty.

Thus, Jefferson would only view the First Amendment through the prism of unalienable rights given by the Creator – a radically theological idea, and his "wall of separation" can have nothing to do with separating religion from political life. It was a reference to his bottom-up Republican view of the federal and state governments, in contrast to the top-down Federalist view.

This being the case, and given our love for metaphors in human communication to sum up something as historically intricate as the First Amendment, what is a positive metaphor to serve its first freedom, of religion, and its cognate four freedoms?

In Genesis 1-2, we find the biblical order of creation. It precedes and defines the fall into sin – best defined as broken trust – which is then introduced in Genesis 3. And the promise of redemption, also introduced in Genesis 3, seeks to restore us to the original good trajectory of the order of creation.

We have two choices in life. Give and it will be given, or take before you are taken. This contest is most importantly a question of power – the power to give versus the power to take. Giving is proactive, taking is reactive.

The only place in written history where the proactive and positive power to give are fully present, and unpolluted by broken trust, war, disease etc., is Genesis 1-2. And here the content of unalienable rights is rooted, even while its language is not technically used – for indeed, "unalienable" is a double negative compound word, and there is no negative to negate in the biblical order of creation. Rather, we have the positive gifts that precede and define the rights we redemptively call unalienable.

Human life is made in the image of God, human freedom is given in the first words to the first man by the sovereign Yahweh Elohim, and we are given the stewardship over the creation to work, produce, prosper and be free in the buying, selling, trading and bartering of our property – all as original gifts of God, and all of which lead to true happiness within the human community in God's sight. Life, liberty, property and the pursuit of happiness.

Crucially here, we have the only proactive definition of human freedom in history. In Genesis 2:15-17, we are given a level playing field to choose between life and death, good and evil, truth and falsehood. The language used here, in the Hebrew, is itself a great metaphor, "in feasting you will continually feast" from an unlimited menu of good choices, versus "in dying you will continually die" if we eat the forbidden fruit.

How many people here tonight do not like the idea of a never-ending banquet to enjoy with your friends and family, with an unlimited menu of good choices? This is the biblical definition of freedom. Thus, we are all theologically united, and I have discovered that the same is true even among pagans and secularists.

This is also the radical nature of the biblical order of creation – nowhere pagan religious origin texts or secular constructs are both good and evil placed side by side, with the freedom given to choose between the two, with the long range confidence that truth will rise to the top, and with the power of the atoning death and resurrection of Jesus to ensure its final possibility for those who believe. This leads us into great and detailed theological territory beyond my available time. But in essence, we cannot be free to say yes to God unless we are first free to say no. This is the freedom of dissent, though we will always reap what we sow. As it says in the RSSV (that is, the Rankin Sub-Standard Version), "God so loved the world that he gave us each the freedom to go to hell if we damn well want to." And I am not using "hell" gratuitously, for as Jesus says, people choose darkness because they know their deeds are evil, and do not want to come into the light, the light that defines the kingdom of God.

One radical element here is that Yahweh Elohim gives the ancient serpent, Satan himself, a level playing field access to the Garden to tempt Adam and Eve. Only truth can get away with such hospitality. As well, the theocracies under the Law of Moses, and under Jesus when he returns, are both communities of choice. There is no such thing as an imposed theocracy in the Bible – "Choose this day whom you will serve" says Joshua.

Jesus follows the same during Passover Week, where he offers a level playing field for his sworn enemies to rake him over the coals with their toughest questions. And by being proven blameless in the process, thus able to die for us as the spotless Lamb of God, the use of the level playing field is the basis for our salvation. Interestingly, when Jesus came into Jerusalem that week as the Son of David, the anointed heir of the founding king of Jerusalem, it is the most explosive church-state debate in history, because of

King Herod the Tetrarch's fears, and of his religious and political sycophants.

The Jewish religious elite had been bought off by Herod the Great from 20 B.C. on following, building them a temple more magnificent than that of Solomon, from whence they derived great wealth and power and status. But it came with a price – they had to agree not to interfere with the Roman political order, to raise questions concerning social justice or mercy outside the temple walls. That was truly a "high and impregnable wall," and Jesus challenged such an idolatry head on. He won the debate hands down, then instead of taking political authority, he suffered and died and rose for us, so we who are Christians are to announce the coming of the true politics, the kingdom of God, using earthly politics to advance religious, political and economic liberty for all people equally, as a taste and invitation to the age to come.

Well, this covers much territory, and we have just skimmed the surface. What can we glean, and what is the positive metaphor we can define?

The reigning metaphor is the "wall of separation between church and state." It is reactive and negative in essence, rooted in the power to take before being taken, and it has been wrongly used since 1947 to restrict religious liberty, where the First Amendment liberties of religious expression have been systematically purged from much of political, governmental, academic and cultural life. And invariably, the cognate First Amendment liberties have also been injured. This purging has been heavily weighted against biblically rooted Christianity. The "wall of separation" language assumes a war, and as such, the war will never end. It separates and does not unify our nation. It is the opposite of *e pluribus unum* – "out of the many, one."

The healthy metaphor would be "a level playing field for all religious and political ideas." In this proactive and positive paradigm, based on the biblical power to give, and rooted in the essence of the Declaration, the checks and balances on power in the Constitution, and in the liberties of the First Amendment, we maximize freedom.

But there is a rub that I suggest lies at the core of the debate. The only Source for these liberties are found in the unalienable rights given by the God of the Bible, and people who do not want to honor the Creator, or who have been burned by impositional religion, fear that an acknowledgement of this Source will permit religionists, especially "Bible thumpers," to shove religion down their throats.

The only Source for unalienable rights is also the only Source for the freedom of religion, and opposition to imposition against the human will is uniquely found in the biblical order of creation. And this is not a partisan religious or institutionally religious sentiment. The biblical order of creation is fully Christian and pre-Christian, fully Jewish and pre-Jewish, fully and universally human, tracing back to the one Creator. As the apostle Paul said to the skeptical Athenians on Mars Hill, "he himself gives all men life and breath and everything else." Therefore, those of us who are truly biblical begin first with the essence of the power to give, which as Jesus taught us, is to treat others as we ourselves wish to be treated. We advance the Gospel in the actions of our lives that honor and do not harm the lives, liberties and properties of others – and thus invite people to consider what they believe, and what best leads to such cherished unalienable rights.

It is a contest of the power to give versus the power to take, and for too long both church and state have majored in the power to take before being taken. The biblical motif is the power to give a level playing field for all ideas to be heard equally, rooted in the Garden of Eden, and with Jesus during Passover Week in the face of his enemies, where first we want to be sure others are listened to before we wish to be heard. This has been the project of the Mars Hill Forums for 14 years now.

We have two choices in life: give and it will be given, or take before you are taken.

And we have two choices of metaphor in American religious and political life: a level playing field versus a wall of separation.

I choose the level playing field, and if enough of the church were to do likewise, the nation would be transformed in the name of Jesus, and more people than ever would be attracted to his person and the kingdom of God into which he invites all of us.

Thank you.

♦ ♦ ♦

Chapter Seven

The Most Important

Ten Commandments Case in the Nation

The issues of a level playing field, unalienable rights and the understanding of church and state swirl around the debate over the Ten Commandments.

But unfortunately, this debate in American politics has revolved around the issue of monuments and public space – in other words, on symbol, not substance. The assumption in a skeptical culture driven by a top-down media is that Christians who want public and historical acknowledgement of the Ten Commandments somehow want to "impose" their religion on everyone else (even though the Commandments are an Israelite and Jewish article of faith first). This reflects a biblical illiteracy. Indeed, the Ten Commandments start with these words, "I am Yahweh your God, who brought you out of Egypt, out of the land of slavery" (Exodus 20:2). The Commandments (literally "words") that follow are words that protect freedom from slavery; the opposite of imposition. This leads to a larger theological discussion of critical importance addressed elsewhere, but for here a crucial question is raised. Are we debating this issue due to mere symbols, or because we care for the true substance of the freedom and life these Commandments were originally meant to serve?

Here in Connecticut, a teacher was fired from a public high school for the mere mention of the Ten Commandments – namely, due to the substance and not merely the symbol. It is, to my knowledge, unique in this regard relative to the more highly publicized disputes on this issue. It is the most important Ten Commandments case in the nation. Due to the way the legal system was structured, there was ample opportunity for the teacher to be denied justice, and as exacerbated by poor legal counsel at critical junctures.

It details how the legal system and education establishment can have little if any interest in honest politics, honest law and a level playing field. Cases like this, on a range of issues, proliferate across the nation where complex and dishonest law tramples religious, political and economic liberty, trapping non-elitists in a labyrinth, surrounded by Medusas at every turn. The only remedy I can see, specifically here in my own experience in seeking to help a friend, and for the nation at large, is a complete reworking of American law rooted in the six pillars of honest politics.

———————————

In 1995, Joyce Sperow, a home economics teacher at Regional 7 High School in Northwestern Connecticut, allowed a student to allude to the Ten Commandments. The context was pedagogical and professional.

Mrs. Sperow was suspended by the School Superintendent for this alleged violation of "church-state" issues. And in a subsequent series of disciplinary hearings and officially sanctioned harassment, she was finally fired for "insubordination" in 2001 – with great loss of income, benefits and pension.

In two hearings and in one lawsuit, Mrs. Sperow was represented by attorneys who failed to win her vindication. In the professional opinions of other attorneys, ex post facto, it was their consensus that she was ill-served by poor counsel or disingenuity.

The centrality of the religious discrimination issue was strenuously avoided by Regional 7, as its attorneys sought to shift the focus to subsequent and non-germane procedural issues. And Mrs. Sperow's attorneys did not challenge this redefinition of the terms.

I helped to counsel Mrs. Sperow across the years, but not being an attorney, I was unable to represent her legally. But had I the time, focus and foresight to press in on the intellectual battles in venues accessible, the result would likely have been different.

Finally Mrs. Sperow appealed to the Connecticut Commission on Human Rights and Opportunities (CHRO) for an "impartial" hearing to see if any discrimination had occurred. The CHRO does not make legal decisions, but based on a review of the facts, with both parties represented, they write a summary opinion. If it is in favor of the plaintiff, a mediation process is offered, and if that fails, then an appeal to the next step in the CHRO process follows.

Mrs. Sperow asked me to serve as her official advocate in the "impartial" hearing, where legal representation was not requisite, so that as a minister, I was able to do so. I sat through some ten hours of meetings on October 15 and 22, 2003 in Waterbury, CT.

As a result of my summary observations and persistent advocacy for the next nine months, on July 15, 2004, the CHRO issued a "Finding of Reasonable Cause" that reversed the prior rulings and found that discrimination had occurred against Mrs. Sperow. The CHRO process indicated a clear bias against Mrs. Sperow from October, 2003 through June, 2004, but facts are stubborn things, and the Finding ended up being a rousing vindication of Mrs. Sperow.

Below is a series of selected communications I had with the CHRO, chronologically ordered, followed by summary observations about the Finding. These communications are like listening to one side of a phone conversation, yet all the details are self-explanatory. As you read through it, you will see how clear the case is on behalf of Mrs. Sperow. These communications assume a mutual familiarity with all the factual details surrounding the case, and *italicized words in brackets are subsequent additions of clarity for the sake of the reader*. At the end of the two fact-finding meetings, I asked the CHRO investigator if I were free to be public about their process and content, and I was told yes (as well, the ten hours were recorded on audiotape as part of the official transcript).

November 20, 2003

To: Ms. Roxanne Sinclair, Esq., Investigator with the CHRO for Case No. 0130607.

Dear Ms. Sinclair:

Serving as an advocate for Mrs. Joyce Sperow, and in attending the Commission's fact finding meetings on October 15 and 22, I observe that the original facts were never investigated. And when I argued this reality during the mediation phase, you dismissed my concerns out of hand.

Here is the simple reality in summation:

1. Dr. Robert Fish [*school superintendent*] stated in the fact finding meeting that Mrs. Sperow has acted "against the law" in a matter of "church-state issues."

2. Dr. Fish never specified what this church-state transgression was.

3. The whole process of Regional 7's actions against Mrs. Sperow began with an accusation that Mrs. Sperow spoke about the "Ten Commandments" with some students (see below), with the implicit understanding that this was an illegal act.

4. In the fact finding meetings, you never investigated this incident, nor questioned Dr. Fish et al. about it.

114

5. The people making this accusation, upon whom Dr. Fish relied, were never identified.

6. The charge against Mrs. Sperow for insubordination is rooted in her refusal to sign a letter written by Dr. Fish, where she was to admit guilt in this matter, and promise never to talk about it. In other words, she was being coerced into perjuring herself, being coerced into breaking the Ninth Commandment.

7. All subsequent complaints of insubordination against Mrs. Sperow are rooted in these unexamined facts.

8. Thus, the CHRO has no basis to reach any judgment in this matter until these facts are investigated.

9. And when these facts are addressed, it is clearly an issue of Mrs. Sperow being denied her First Amendment liberties in matters of religion and speech. The question of "insubordination" is an ex post facto ruse to avoid this reality.

10. If Mrs. Sperow is to be disciplined for the mention of the Ten Commandments, then Regional 7 is to be found likewise guilty before the fact. Namely, by displaying a menorah in the school, they have profiled, in pedagogical context for all students and faculty, the representation of the candelabrum that historically stood next to the stone engravings of the Ten Commandments in the Ark of the Covenant, in the inner sanctuary of the Jewish Temple in Jerusalem.

Therefore, the CHRO deliberately did not investigate these original and determinative facts of the case. You have not fulfilled your duties. Mrs. Sperow has suffered religious discrimination, Dr. Fish et al. have sought to hide behind claims of authority and means of procedure, and you have given aid to their agenda, thus serving to "bear false witness," i.e., to willfully violate the Ninth Commandment. Or in other words, you have confirmed by your actions that the whole matter is one of freedom of religion and speech with respect to the pedagogical use of the Ten Commandments to show students that it is wrong to lie.

The above facts have also been ignored by Regional 7's attorney, Mark J. Sommaruga, in his November 3 post fact finding brief.

1. The October 15 and 22 CHRO fact finding meetings are demonstrably not "impartial" as they were supposed to be [*as Mr. Sommaruga claimed*]. The original and determinative facts were not investigated, and moreover, they were dismissed out of hand when I sought to raise them on Mrs. Sperow's behalf.

2. The Establishment Clause of the First Amendment was never investigated either. The predicate for liberty of speech, press, assembly and redress of grievances is rooted in the prior liberty of religion. Without the liberty to believe freely, there is no liberty to speak what you believe, publish what you believe, assemble on the basis of your beliefs, or redress the government based on your beliefs.

3. Mr. Sommaruga says there is "absolutely no proof" that the actions against Mrs. Sperow were on the basis of her "religious status." That is a curious clause, as though religious belief is determined by "status" (i.e., "class"), and not individual liberty that is status and class neutral. Rather, Mr. Sommaruga, by also ignoring the original and determinative facts of the case, has refused to investigate the religious liberty issue. At the fact finding hearing, he dismissed the matter up front as you did in the mediation process.

4. Thus, both the CHRO and Mr. Sommaruga are partial by refusal to investigate what "church-state issue" Dr. Fish accused Mrs. Sperow of violating. The very issue that set this whole process into motion.

Most sincerely,

Rev. John C. Rankin

cc: Mrs. Joyce Sperow; Atty. Mark J. Sommaruga

Salient facts as I submitted to the CHRO on October 15 (*2003*):

1. The initial charge [*in September, 1995*] against Mrs. Sperow is rooted in religious discrimination – a charge that her mere mention of the "Ten Commandments" was unacceptable behavior for a public school teacher.

a. The situation at hand began with some female students making noise outside her classroom door during lunch period. Mrs. Sperow spoke with them, as they stepped inside the door adjacent to her classroom, and asked why they were not in the cafeteria as they were supposed to be. They said they were waiting for another teacher. Mrs. Sperow knew this to be untrue, that the teacher in question was in the cafeteria. Instead of confronting the students with a mere charge that they were lying, Mrs. Sperow sought a diplomatic route. She sought to help the girls to come to such a conclusion on their own, and thus make this a "teachable" moment that would increase their true dignity and capacity as moral agents. Mrs. Sperow then used a point of common reference – a "Get Acquainted" class the prior year where these girls had introduced some of their background. Mrs. Sperow asked them if they remembered the "Get Acquainted" class, and they said yes. In that class, the girls spoke of the specific church they attended, of their own initiative. Mrs. Sperow responded by asking them what they learned at their church, and they mentioned the "Creed," the "Our Father," and the "Ten Commandments." So now Mrs. Sperow then asked, "Do you think there is one Commandment that applies to this situation?" They responded, "Thou shalt not lie."

Thus, Mrs. Sperow took information provided by the students, as rooted in a history between she and them that honors the established protocol for religious liberty in a public school setting. She used it with wise diplomacy, and succeeded in getting the girls to admit their own lying at the moment. Mrs. Sperow should be commended for this tact. But instead she has been systematically harassed by Regional 7 officials, catalyzed by reaction to her effective handling of the situation.

2. This harassment involved four disciplinary hearings [*between 1996 and 2001*] aimed at Mrs. Sperow.

a. In the first hearing, Dr. Robert Fish asked Mrs. Sperow to sign a statement agreeing to the merit of a 10-day suspension being imposed on her; and also her agreement not to mention the nature of the suspension to anyone else. In other words, she was being asked to lie because she successfully taught some students that lying was wrong, and to lie by covering up the putative reason for her suspension. Two different attorneys advised Mrs. Sperow not to sign such a false agreement. Because of her refusal to perjure herself, Mrs. Sperow was charged with "insubordination."

b. A second hearing focused on two incidents. The first occurred in a cooking class, where there were groups of students in four different kitchens. One group was unruly, and as one female member of the group went to a common area, she was about to place a wrong item in one of the recycling bins. Mrs. Sperow lifted the lid, and said to her: "Read this – what does it say?" The girl charged Mrs. Sperow with being unkind, and said she felt unhappy about Mrs. Sperow coming so close to her so as to have her right hand brush against the student's arm.

The second occurred when Mrs. Sperow once asked a female student to close the cupboard door, and in the process brushed the student's elbow. The girl screeched, "Don't touch me!"

118

Accordingly, an edict was given by Regional 7 for Mrs. Sperow not to touch any students.

c. The third hearing was called in a reprise concerning touching students [*concluding sentence below here excised*]. During study hall one day, one male student was showing a photo album to some female students. They were giggling and not settling into class. So Mrs. Sperow told the girls to go to their seats, and for the boy to put the photo album away. The girls said "No." So Mrs. Sperow said, "I will keep the album on the desk until the end of the period," after which the boy was free to pick it up. He complied. But the girls then came to take the album off the desk. So Mrs. Sperow put it in her backpack, reading aloud from the student handbook the specific rules for classroom behavior she was enforcing. Several girls surrounded her to distract her while another girl sought to reach into Mrs. Sperow's backpack to extract the album. Simultaneously, Mrs. Sperow placed her hand down upon [*her own*] backpack to prevent this, and as it happens, came into contact with the student's hand seeking to reach into the backpack. The student claimed she was "slapped."

Thus, Mrs. Sperow was again reprimanded for "insubordination."

d. The fourth hearing was called in response to yet another incident. In a study hall for unruly male students, one boy was seeking by creative means (crawling under desks etc.) to escape the classroom in order to wander the halls. Mrs. Sperow twice returned him to his desk, as he complied with the verbal order, but then had to put him in her office to keep it from happening again. He sat in her chair, which had wheels on it, and was rolling in and out of the doorway, yelling at the other students. Mrs. Sperow told him he must be quiet, and in response, he slammed the office door shut. When he tried to open it from within, he was unable, and thus he had to sit in the office another fifteen minutes until the end of the class. He was compliant [*a claim that was later challenged*], and Mrs. Sperow let him out accordingly. But in the subsequent class he attended, he told fellow students of the incident, some of those students reported it to the administration, and Mrs. Sperow was charged with "imprisoning" the student.

As is evident, all these incidents are rooted in unruly and rebellious students lying about Mrs. Sperow as she sought to gain a modicum of control in the hallway and classroom. Her actions were all restrained and professional. Yet Mrs. Sperow had many burdensome rules placed upon her in the process, with no precedent even among teachers who were in genuine need of discipline. In fact, Mrs. Sperow was regularly assigned the most unruly students to monitor, and instead of thanks, she was harassed. [*Also, Mrs. Sperow had other teachers assigned to sit in her classroom from time to time to "monitor" her.*]

In my October 15 summation of the facts, I was unaware of the Hutterian Brethren incident, thus I added these comments on October 22:

In the incident where Mrs. Sperow called the Hutterian Brethren anonymously [*relative to the possible religious harassment of some of their children, seeking evidence bolstering her own case*], Mrs. Sperow was wrong [*in making the call anonymously, out of her own fear*], and has apologized. Reconciliation in such matters as these include the professional willingness of any and all to admit error when it is shown. Nonetheless, this error on Mrs. Sperow's part was an error of reaction to the "hostile environment" she was subjected to, as she sought to protect herself; and not out of any initiative against another person.

120

April 14, 2004

To: Ms. Roxanne Sinclair, Esq., Investigator with the CHRO for Case No. 0130607.

Dear Ms. Sinclair:

Last October 22, you expressed resolve, as the end of the Commission's fact finding process, to rule on Mrs. Joyce Sperow's case by the end of the calendar year if not sooner.

It is mid-April, and you have never been in contact with me as Mrs. Sperow's advocate, and only in passing on two detail matters with Mrs. Sperow.

When may we expect to receive from you a detailed answer to my letter of November 20? A copy is enclosed.

Most sincerely,

Rev. John C. Rankin

cc: Mrs. Joyce Sperow; Atty. Mark J. Sommaruga

April 28, 2004

To: Ms. Pekah Wallace, Regional Manager for the CHRO.

[Here Ms. Wallace had signed a cover letter approving the Draft Reasonable Cause Finding of April 19, and I mistakenly thought she had written it instead of Ms. Sinclair who actually wrote it. I did not discover this mistake until a later review.]

Dear Ms. Wallace:

I am in receipt of the Draft Reasonable Cause Finding re: CHRO No.: 0130607 – Sperow vs. Regional School District No. 7; EEOC No.: 15aa3360. Thank you.

And I understand that Atty. Mark Sommaruga must respond by May 4, if he can sustain an objection to your summary of the facts, and your determination that reasonable cause exists for believing a discriminatory act has occurred against Mrs. Sperow.

As her advocate, and at this juncture, I would like to add one additional perspective.

Namely, whereas the Finding acknowledges the presence of religious discrimination, it focuses on itemizing elements of age and sex discrimination. Now age and sex discrimination are properly in view, but they are also secondary in nature. With respect to my November 20, 2003 ten-point outline of the facts of the case, your Finding of course does not dispute them, but neither does it focus on them. It is Mrs. Sperow's belief, and I agree with her, that religious discrimination is the overwhelming and defining reality. It is an egregious failure of the system, and of Mrs. Sperow's prior legal representation, that this reality was so often pushed aside. And in my presence, Attys. Roxanne Sinclair and Sommaruga likewise sought to dismiss it. Thus, in whatever lies before us in the process of winning full justice for Mrs. Sperow, the salient centrality of religious discrimination remains our concern.

Most sincerely,

Rev. John C. Rankin

cc: Mrs. Joyce Sperow; Atty. Mark J. Sommaruga

———————————

May 8, 2004

To: Ms. Pekah Wallace, Regional Manager for the CHRO.

Dear Ms. Wallace:

I am in receipt of Atty. Mark J. Sommaruga's May 3, 2004 [*38 page*] response to your April, 19, 2004 Draft Reasonable Cause Finding re: CHRO No.: 0130607 – Sperow vs. Regional School District No. 7; EEOC No.: 15aa3360.

In his response, Mr. Sommaruga only confirms the ten-point factual summary I submitted on November 20, 2003, with attendant commentary, and my reiteration of the centrality of religious discrimination in my April 28 letter to you (copies enclosed).

Namely, his argument is rooted in ex post facto matters relative to the original facts concerning religious discrimination. These are facts he never addresses, facts that remain uncontested. Thus, all the argumentation he marshals is materially irrelevant until he is able to contest and sustain an objection to these original facts.

Most sincerely,

Rev. John C. Rankin

cc: Mrs. Joyce Sperow; Atty. Mark J. Sommaruga

June 7, 2004

To: Ms. Roxanne Sinclair, Esq., Investigator with the CHRO; re: Mrs. Joyce Sperow: CHRO Case 0130607; EEOC Case 15aa3360.

Dear Ms. Sinclair:

Thank you for your phone call this morning.

Whereas you do not wish to commit our conversation to writing, I will do so in salient summary. I understand the following:

1. You wish that Mrs. Sperow had an attorney representing her before the CHRO, with an implicit sense, as I judged it, that it would better serve her than an advocate who is not an attorney.

2. The final summary is not yet complete, and you do not yet know its conclusion.

3. Though [*your*] draft summary ruled there is reasonable cause that Mrs. Joyce Sperow suffered discrimination, you state that it is a weak case.

4. You invited me to propose a settlement in the interim, and you outlined some of its parameters.

5. You stated that you want me to do this as soon as possible, due to deadlines or pressures you face.

6. I gave you a 10-14 day range to give a response, and you tried to insist I do it sooner.

7. You promised you would contact me in this time period if there were any impending deadline(s) of which I must be aware.

Here are some current observations and questions:

1. As I stated in my November 20, 2003 letter, and again in my April 28 and May 8 letters, the original facts concerning the religious discrimination were never investigated by your office, and you explicitly denied there was any [*apart from your draft summary that does acknowledge*] religious discrimination explicitly but briefly, [*turning your*] attention [*instead*] to secondary concerns of age and sex discrimination [*in great detail*]. But religious discrimination is the paramount reality, and neither you nor Mr.

124

Sommaruga has challenged any of the facts I presented in this vein. Your office cannot be impartial in its role unless all of the facts I have presented are examined, and detailed in writing on your part. Namely – am I right in those facts, or am I in error? And if it is the latter, what are your contrary factual claims?

2. I see an unmistakable pattern to avoid the religious discrimination reality, [*as you acknowledge it only in one clause, and studiously avoid it otherwise, and for Mr. Sommaruga*], I see more than avoidance – I see tautological denial ( ). Indeed, in Mrs. Sperow's prior legal counsel, this avoidance was also in play. Only now that I have itemized it after sitting in on the CHRO fact finding meetings, as her chosen advocate, has even a favorable draft opinion come Mrs. Sperow's way. You may think the draft summary is weak in terms of age and sex discrimination, but you have yet to deal with the strength of my advocacy concerning religious discrimination.

3. After the October 22 CHRO meeting, you asked me and Mr. Sommaruga to prepare our written arguments within a month's time. You stated that you were under some time constraints, and you intended to issue a ruling in early [*to mid*] December. I did so by November 20, but then I heard nothing from you by mid-April. So I wrote you a letter on April 14 inquiring why, and then [*you*] issued the draft summary on April 19, footnoting my April 14 letter. If you were under such time constraints as earlier indicated, why the four-month delay?

4. Thus, why should I have cause to consider there is a real time constraint now? If there is, I need to know exactly what it is, and what jeopardy Mrs. Sperow might be under if a certain timetable is required by law. I shall be as prompt as my schedule allows, with certain variables beyond my full control factored in.

Most sincerely,

Rev. John C. Rankin

cc: Mrs. Joyce Sperow; Ms. Pekah Wallace; Atty. Mark J. Sommaruga

---

There was no direct reply to this letter from Ms. Sinclair. Then with her July 15, 2004 "Finding of Reasonable Cause," I was happily astonished at how complete and resounding the vindication for Mrs. Sperow was. Consider this sequence:

1. The CHRO investigator, Ms. Roxanne Sinclair, Esq., stated in the October 22, 2003 mediation phase that there was no religious discrimination involved, as the attorney for Regional 7, Mr. Mark J. Sommaruga, Esq., maintained to the end.

2. In my November 20, 2003 letter to the CHRO with a summary of the original facts, I showed completely otherwise.

3. In the CHRO Draft Summary of April 19, 2004, Ms. Sinclair admitted religious discrimination in one clause only, but then itemized data relative only to age and sex discrimination, valid albeit secondary elements.

4. In my April 28 response to the Draft Summary, I reiterated the centrality of the original facts of religious discrimination.

5. In my May 8 response to Mr. Sommaruga's May 3 rebuttal of the Draft Summary, I reiterated the same again.

6. In her June 7 phone call to me, Ms. Sinclair tried to move me off the case by ostensibly wishing Mrs. Sperow had legal representation instead, even though, and as a minister, I was the only one who had produced positive results for Mrs. Sperow so far. Ms. Sinclair said

that the Draft Summary case for Mrs. Sperow was "weak," with reference, I believe, to the secondary elements of age and sex.

7. In response, I again reiterated and strengthened the case for the original facts of religious discrimination, noting the pattern of avoidance on Ms. Sinclair's part, and of tautological denial on Mr. Sommaruga's part.

8. In the July 15 Final Finding, Ms. Sinclair radically and abruptly changed focus. It was not organized in a chronological pattern of starting with the original facts, then examining cause and effect – as I wished to see. It was still locked in ex post facto procedural mode, yet even there, in the text and footnotes, she finally addressed the original facts, at least in an overview capacity, and strengthened them somewhat with material I found secondary, and also strengthened the age and sex discrimination factors. As well, Ms. Sinclair's ruling contained additional language of rebuke for School Superintendent Dr. Fish's vindictive agenda against Mrs. Sperow.

Here are some salient quotes from the Final Finding:

- "The respondent [*Regional 7*] denied any and all claims of discrimination and, specifically, any claims of discrimination on the basis of age or religious belief" (p. 2).
- "The investigator proceeded to conduct a thorough and complete investigation…" (p. 3).
- "Is the respondent's explanation credible? No" (p. 6).
- "A comparison of the complainant's [*Mrs. Sperow's*] first suspension in September 1995, for violation of so-called Church/State issues … showed (that) … there were no clearly established rules setting standards for the alleged misconduct" (p. 7).

- "In contrast, the complainant was suspended for two weeks for so-called Church/State issues. The respondent had no rules or policy defining Church/State issues. The incidents were not related to repeat occurrences. No evidence was ever offered by respondent of any investigation into the specific conduct at issue in each instance" (p. 8).
- "The anonymous phone call to the Hutterian Brethren was the only incident investigated" (p. 8).
- "Why did Dr. Fish regard this as a Church/State issue?" (p. 8).
- "Why did Dr. Fish regard this as a Church/State issue?" (again, on p. 8).
- "Fish did not disclose the source of the alleged complaint" (p. 8).
- "How did Dr. Fish conclude that both instances were Church/State issues?" (p. 8).
- "Fish blew up when she refused to sign agreeing to discipline that she in principle did not agree with and when she failed to sign it he took deliberate action to fire her" (p. 9, footnote 6).
- "Fish's attempt to fire her was a vindictive act" (p. 9, footnote 7).
- "There is no indication that sexual harassment or physically abusive contact was at issue here. Most of the incidents of alleged 'unwanted touching' were vague and unsubstantiated" (p. 9, footnote 8).
- "The sequence of events arguably supports the complainant's claim she was being pressured to retire as part of an overall pattern of disciplinary harassment by Dr. Fish and the respondent Board of Education" (p. 11).
- "The offer is in Dr. Fish's handwriting. The complainant was not invited to meet with him in his office to discuss the offer. The offer

128

was not presented through the complainant's union. In fact, he insisted on meeting her away from the school" (p. 11).

- "Is the proof in the investigative file, considered in its entirety, sufficient to support a finding that there does exist reasonable cause to believe that illegal discrimination has occurred? Yes" (p. 12).

Despite this ruling, Regional 7 was not amenable to any just settlement. Thus, an appeals process within the CHRO was automatically followed, and this time, it was required for Mrs. Sperow to have legal representation. I secured for her excellent counsel. Mrs. Sperow had a prior ruling against her in Superior Court, when she was represented by an attorney who did not represent her well or according to her wishes that the case be a matter of religious liberty, not procedure. Because of this loss in court, *res judicata* was now applied at the CHRO final hearing, and it brought to an end this avenue of appeal for Mrs. Sperow.

Mrs. Sperow's options since have been a) to file a lawsuit in the State Supreme Court, or b) to file a lawsuit in the Second District the U.S. Court of Appeals. But she does not have the money. I clearly see it as a First Amendment case, and now that it is out of the CHRO orb, all parties involved in the original CHRO hearing may be deposed.

Present advice of legal counsel says that these options are very difficult to pursue within the current legal system, apart from some remarkable public pressure. Legislative change is necessary to prevent future such injustices.

◆ ◆ ◆

Chapter Eight

A Biblical Alternative to Health Insurance

With the travesty of imposed healthcare, whether at the state level with RomneyCare, or federally with ObamaCare, it hangs over the economy, physicians and patients like the Sword of Damocles. Here is a simple alternative, where as necessary, it will be advanced through the insistence pof First Amendment religious liberty. As a physician's son, I have cared about this issue deeply for a long time.

TEI Burden Sharing
Simplicity and Trust in Medical Care

www.teiburdensharing.com

Summation

Historically, the Amish people take care of each other's burdensome needs, including healthcare. No legal contracts or complexities – just simple trust, rooted in a shared culture in geographical proximity.

Is such a model of trust possible nationwide? Yes – for those of us who embrace a simple covenant:

1. We affirm the goodness of the biblical order of creation. Here, a healthy social order is rooted in the marriage of one man and one woman in mutual fidelity.

2. In addressing health needs, the stewardship of our bodies is best served by what is most naturally present in the biblical order of creation.

3. On this basis, we pool our resources to meet each other's burdensome healthcare needs, where an honest and open business model is in place.

4. Thus, healthcare quality will be far higher, and costs will be far lower.

Once this plan is well underway, with proven demographics, a second plan is envisioned for people who do not affirm the biblical order of creation, but who want a similar simple system.

Specific Guidelines

TEI Burden Sharing pools the monies of its members to share burdensome medical expenses. It does so based on mutual trust in complete transparency, with a simple moral covenant as opposed to a written legal contract. It reduces costs dramatically, and multiplies quality care.

Members of TEI Burden Sharing embrace the following six ethics:

1. Truth telling.

2. Trust and simplicity are the basis for a healthy life, and rooted in the biblical order of creation.

3. Trust and simplicity are first and best nurtured where human sexuality equals chastity outside of heterosexual faithful monogamous marriage, fidelity within, and parenthood based thereupon; where human life is affirmed fully from natural conception to natural death.

4. Healthy living includes no use of inhaled tobacco, illegal drugs or substances; and no abuse of legal drugs, substances or alcoholic beverages.

5. Healthy living means the pursuit of a wise diet, always preferring food and drink in their most natural state, of appropriate exercise, outdoor air and sunshine, and sufficient rest.

6. Healthy living gives deliberate priority to a philosophy of proactively strengthening the body's natural self-healing processes; and only as a last resort to reactively remove ill health by means of pharmaceuticals, surgery, radiation etc. Specifically, preventative measures are always embraced, and then the simplest, most natural and direct treatments for specific illnesses are embraced.

TEI Burden Sharing is run by the Theological Education Institute (TEI), LLC, with the following nine guidelines:

1. Members are interviewed, affirm the six ethics, and come to an agreement on their budgetable and burdensome medical expenses, and their monthly contribution to the pool.

2. Monies are contributed monthly by all, and paid out monthly to those in need. Three months of contributions are due up front for the membership to become active. This is for initial overhead. After that, the contribution of every twelfth month is for regular overhead, with the prior eleven months going into the pooled medical expenses account.

3. The overhead account and medical account are strictly separate and the funds will never commingle; the records of all income, expenses and current amount of monies in the medical account will always be available to members, online, by email and/or otherwise.

4. When members need to have medical expenses paid, they contact their Advocate, and it will be processed promptly. If there are excess monies in the medical account at the end of the month, they will remain there for the subsequent month(s).

5. If there is a shortage, special gifts will be solicited from the membership; if there still remains a shortage at the end of the calendar month, the due ratio (e.g., 95%) of all needs will be paid, and thus, the medical account will never go into the negative, and never carry any future debt to its members.

6. Members are free to choose their health care providers, and as well, TEI Burden Sharing will build a professional list of member physicians and heath care providers whom it will recommend.

7. Members are free to discontinue membership at anytime, but will have to reach a new agreement in order to rejoin; those who fall short in their monthly giving will have to discontinue their membership or renegotiate a new agreement.

8. Any issues of disputed concern between members are to be handled according to Matthew 18:15-17.

9. TEI Burden Sharing, being a moral covenant, and not a legal contract, does not pretend to carry any legal indemnification.

If you wish to join such a covenant, email **tei@teii.org** and let us know.

Chapter Nine
Simplified State Law

Based on the six pillars of honest politics as translated into appropriate context, the power of a level playing field, the power of checks and balances, and via the power of Occam's razor, here is a detailed proposal that reduces the Connecticut Constitution and General Statutes from 17,000 pages to little more than 33. The result can serve justice and mercy for all people equally, rooted in an easily accessible and understandable legal code, and most attractive to the overwhelming majority of voters. Or to put it another way: simplicity, truth telling and transparency in politics. And a template can be made available for all other states.

The United States is a federation of 13 states originally, and now fifty. The U.S. Constitution seeks to highlight state's rights, where the federal government is meant to protect their freedoms as much as possible, and thus protecting such a federation from threats without and within. The federal government was designed originally not to interfere with life, liberty and property as protected by the states, and later through the Fourteenth Amendment, to proactively assure such protection, yet always in the process to devolve as much decision making power to the states, and the states to their local municipalities. Initially the equation was in the reverse order – local municipalities granted limited jurisdiction to the states, which granted limited jurisdiction to the federal government. But government has grown so large, and law so huge and labyrinthine that we must now reverse the reversal, and speak of devolving power back to where it belongs. Trust is best nurtured among people who know each other, thus the need is to devolve law to the most local level possible.

The place to start this project is at the state level, where decision-making power is devolved back to the municipalities as appropriate. Here I submit a proposal for my home state, Connecticut, a working draft. Once this occurs at the state level, it becomes easier to accomplish it at the federal level.

The Constitution and General Laws of the State of Connecticut
(Proposed Revision © 2012 John C. Rankin)

Preamble

We the people of Connecticut, in order to establish a just, peaceful and prosperous state, establish this Constitution and General Laws.

We make six assumptions that serve the consent of the governed, and thus an honest political state.

First, the unalienable rights of life, liberty and property, given by the Creator, belong to all people equally, and leaders in state government honor such rights.

Second, leaders in state government are to be fully transparent in all manners related to the public trust.

Third, an honest definition of terms in necessary in state government, providing a level playing field for all ideas to be heard equally, apart from which political freedom is not possible.

Fourth, leaders in state government are to honor and answer those who pose them the toughest questions.

Fifth, leaders in state government are to respect the common humanity of even the harshest of political opponents.

Sixth, in the face of our individual and societal transgressions against each other, leaders in state government are to work toward justice and reconciliation.

We embrace the most localized and limited government possible, with built in checks and balances, and where simplicity and truth are seen as partners. Accordingly, the maximum discretion of private citizens to organize their social space benefits society the best.

Article I
Declaration of Rights

Section 1:1: When people form a social compact, all are equal in rights, and none are entitled to special or hereditary privileges from the community. All people are made in God's image, and are to be protected by due process of law for the entire natural duration of their lives.

Section 1:2: The social compact is dependent on the prior integrity of man and woman in marriage insofar as attainable, and on the fullest presence possible of both father and mother in the raising of children.

Section 1:3: All political power is inherent in the people, and all free governments are founded on their authority and instituted for their benefit. The people have at all times an undeniable right to alter their form of government as they see fit.

Section 1:4: Religious liberty is the first freedom, where the state cannot define religion, nor can any religious group define the state. Then there follows the freedoms of speech, the press, peaceable assembly, and the power of the people to petition the government for a redress of grievances.

Section 1:5: Every citizen has a right to bear arms in defense of himself, his family, his community and the state. The people are secure in their persons, houses, papers, communications and possessions from unreasonable searches and seizures, by any means. No warrant to search any person, place or thing, or to seize any property, is issued apart from a reasonably specific description, or without probable cause supported by oath or affirmation.

Section 1:6: No one may be deprived of life, liberty or property apart from due process of law. Innocence is presumed until guilt is proven. If property is deemed necessary for the public trust, a just and fair market compensation, including relocation costs, must be provided first.

Section 1:7: All courts are open to every person for speedy redress of any injury done him in his person, property or reputation, rooted in a justice not for sale.

Section 1:8: In all criminal prosecutions, the accused has the right 1) to be heard by himself and counsel, 2) to be informed of the nature and probable cause of the accusation, 3) to be confronted by the witnesses against him, 4) to have the power to subpoena witnesses on his behalf, 5) to be released on bail upon sufficient security, except in capital offenses where the proof is evident or the presumption great, 6) to a speedy and public trial by jury, 7) not to be forced to give evidence against himself, 8) not to be subject to excessive bail or fines, and 9) no civilian criminal prosecutions will be levied against soldiers in the army or militia when in actual service in time of war or public danger.

Section 1:9: In all criminal prosecutions, a victim has the right 1) to be treated with fairness and respect, 2) to timely disposition of the case, 3) to be reasonably protected from the accused, 4) to notification of court proceedings, 5) to attend all court proceedings where the accused is expected to attend, apart from when the victim's testimony will be materially affected by other testimony, 6) to communicate with the prosecution, 7) to make a statement in court in objection to or support of any plea agreement reached by the accused and prosecution, 8) to make a statement in court at sentencing, 9) to a minimum of full restitution of loss caused by the accused, and 10) to information about the arrest, conviction, sentence, imprisonment and release of the accused.

Section 1:10: The privileges of the writ of habeas corpus are not suspended, unless, when in the case of rebellion or invasion, the public safety may require it, and then, only by a vote of two-thirds of the Legislature. The Legislature has no power to impose a bill of attainder for treason or felony. The military is in all cases and at all times subject to the civil power. No soldier, in time of peace, is to be quartered in any house or dwelling without the consent of the owner or legal resident, nor quartered in time of war apart from a manner prescribed by law.

Section 1:11: The right to trial by jury is inviolate, and apart from the consent of the accused, involving no less than six jurors, and in cases of capital offense, no less than twelve jurors. In all cases, the parties have the right to peremptorily challenge jurors to a number established by law or consent, and the right to question each juror individually by counsel is inviolate.

Section 1:12: Any rights not here specified, and not in conflict with those otherwise delineated at the state or federal level, are reserved to the people.

Article II
Separation of Powers

Section 2:1: The powers of government are separated into three divisions, each with their own jurisdiction – the Legislative, the Executive and the Judicial. The Legislative, on its own terms, may delegate regulatory authority to the Executive.

Section 2:2: The Legislative adopts laws to be listed in the General Statutes, which require a two-thirds vote, and are vote on integrally, without amendment. Or the Legislative may adopt designated directives due to exigency, based on specified constitutional or statutory precedence, by majority vote, of 100 words or less, and recorded in the annals of the state department responsible for their enforcement. Each constitutional officer state department has the power to make similar directives under its purview, which are enacted when and if the General Assembly approves them by majority vote. All General Assembly directives are by definition subcategories of laws, and included duly under reference to law.

Section 2:3: The Judiciary only decides matters before it according to constitutional language and scope, and likewise in accord with the Federal Constitution as the case may require.

Article III
The Legislative

Section 3:1: Legislative power is vested in two distinct houses, the House of Representatives and the Senate, and both together as the General Assembly, and is a part-time legislature. It has sole authority for passing law.

Section 3:2: The General Assembly alone has the power to tax, all taxes must be in fair proportion to government's legitimate needs, must be derived from productive economic activity, and must encourage entrepreneurial ventures and capital formation for businesses and job creation.

Section 3:3: The House and Senate each set their own protocol for the conduct of the people's business and on the state website will publish it calendar, in summary and detail, with ample advance notice of any public hearings or votes. Any legislator who takes an action that is properly in the public domain, but is not disclosed, is subject to reprimand or removal by the General Assembly.

Section 3:4: The regular session of the General Assembly convenes in Hartford, beginning on the second Tuesday in January, and adjourning no later than the end of the second Tuesday in May. The Governor may convene a special session of the General Assembly at a time and place deemed appropriate for special emergencies, for up to three calendar days.

Section 3:5: The Senate is composed of thirty members, each member being at least twenty-one years of age and an elector who primarily resides in the senatorial district he represents. There is one Senator for each district, a district that first is to be the most naturally defined and contiguous territory radiating from the heaviest population center, and second, as reasonably equal in population with all other districts as such natural boundaries accord, never splitting any municipality insofar as possible, never splitting any precinct.

Section 3:6: The House of Representatives is composed of one hundred and twenty members, each member being at least twenty-one years of age and an elector who primarily resides in the representative district he represents. There is one Representative for each district, a district that first is to be the most naturally defined and contiguous territory radiating from the heaviest population center, and second, as reasonably equal in population with all other districts as such natural boundaries accord, never splitting any municipality except when its size exceeds possibility, insofar as possible, and never splitting precincts. Each senatorial district exactly equals four most naturally contiguous representative districts.

Section 3:7: U.S. Congressional districts, consistent with federal constitutional standards, are first to be the most naturally defined and contiguous territory radiating from the heaviest population center, and second, as reasonably equal in population with all other districts as such natural boundaries accord, and never splitting any municipalities.

Section 3:8: When and if the federal government increases or decreases the number of congressional districts, the General Assembly determines reapportionment by a two-thirds vote, consistent with federal and state standards.

Section 3:9: The Treasurer, the Secretary of the State and Comptroller canvass publicly the votes for the Representatives and Senators. The person who gains the majority or largest plurality of votes is declared as duly elected in each district, and confirmed as such on the first day of the next legislative session.

Section 3:10: The public election for members of the General Assembly is held on the first Tuesday following the first Monday of November in even-numbered years. Members hold their offices from the convening of the first session following their election, until their successors are duly qualified. Vacancies that occur in the intervening period are filled by a special election at a time determined by the General Assembly.

Section 3:11: Votes by the electors for members of the General Assembly are collected by the presiding officers in the several towns and cities, tallied in specificity, with a copy delivered to the town or city clerk within three days, and under seal to the Secretary of the State within ten days.

Section 3:12: The House of Representatives chooses a speaker, clerk and other officers The Senate chooses a President pro tempore, clerk and other officers, except the President. A majority in each House constitutes a quorum to do business, but ten percent may adjourn and compel the attendance of absent members to gain a quorum.

Section 3:13: Each House determines its own rules and proceedings, and may expel a member for original cause with a two-thirds vote. Each House conducts its assemblies and debates in public, and publishes a journal of all of its proceedings, also available on the state's website; except when a two-thirds majority may require an element kept secret for the sake of state security or for protecting innocent parties. All contracts with public or private concerns are made in open meetings, including all bidding processes, and with full access to the media.

Section 3:14: Members of the General Assembly are privileged from arrest in all cases of civil process during any session and for four days prior and subsequent, except for treason, felony and breach of peace, and are accountable for their speech in the assembly, but in no other place. The salary and expenses of the members of the General Assembly are determined by law, with any changes only effective subsequent to the next election, and no member of the General Assembly is at the same time to hold any other position in local, state or federal government.

Section 3:15: The House of Representatives has the sole power of impeachment. All impeachments are tried by the Senate, sealed by oath or affirmation, conviction requires at least a two-thirds vote of those present, and in the case of the Governor being impeached, the Chief Justice presides. Executive and judicial officers are liable to impeachment, but judgments do not extend past removal from office and further disqualifications to hold any office of honor, trust or profit under the state. Nonetheless, convicted parties remain liable and subject to indictment, trial and punishment according to law. Treason against the state consists only of levying war against it, or in giving aid and comfort to its enemies, and only upon the testimony of at least two witnesses to the same overt act, or confession in open court; no conviction of treason, or attainder, may corrupt blood relationships.

Section 3:16: Unless otherwise stipulated in the General Statutes, and consistent with the same, the U.S. Constitution and the Connecticut Constitution, the definitions, scope and limitation of any and all crimes, civil or criminal, means of evidence, their means of prosecution or vindication, are defined by the General Assembly within the three arenas they occur, against the life, liberty or property of another person, other persons, or against the state.

Article IV
The Executive

Section 4:1: The public election for the Governor, Lieutenant Governor, Treasurer, Secretary of the State, Comptroller and Attorney General is held on the first Tuesday following the first Monday of November, 2012, and every four years thereafter. Such constitutional officers hold their respective offices from the second Tuesday of January succeeding their election, and until their successors are duly qualified. If any member of the executive takes any action that is properly in the public domain but done without due transparency, he is subject to reprimand or removal by a three-quarters vote of the General Assembly.

Section 4:2: The Governor and Lieutenant Governor are elected as a unit, and will appear likewise on all ballots. Votes by the electors for constitutional officers are collected by the presiding officers in the several towns and cities, tallied in specificity, with a copy delivered to the town or city clerk within three days, and under seal to the Secretary of the State within ten days. The Governor and Lieutenant Governor must each be an elector in the state, and at least thirty years of age. Compensation for the

Governor and Lieutenant Governor is established by law, with any changes only effective subsequent to the next election of the same.

The supreme executive power of the state is vested in the Governor who takes care that the laws are faithfully executed. The Governor is a full-time position, and he oversees all matters of the executive branch. As with all constitutional officers, the Governor may issue policy directives of 100 words or less, subject each to approval of the General Assembly, and they are to be debated and defined in public meetings. His contracts with public or private concerns are made in open meetings, including all bidding processes, and with full access to the media.

The Governor's cabinet consists of all department secretaries, who give advice on all matters of protocol, staffing, commissions etc., in the Governor's service to the people's business. The Governor and cabinet will meet together in person no less than once a month, excepting July or August as they themselves choose. All commissions are to be in the name and by the authority of the State of Connecticut, sealed with the state seal, signed by the Governor, and attested by the Secretary of the State.

The Governor is in charge of all emergency resources for the state, and in consultation with his cabinet, has the power to define, declare and rescind a state of emergency. The Governor nominates members for the Supreme Court, subject to approval by the Senate.

The Governor is captain general of the state militia, except when called into service to the United States. He may require information in writing or orally, and if need be, in public assembly, from any of all of the constitutional officers and members of the Supreme Court, on any subject relative to the duties of their respective offices. He may adjourn the General Assembly in the event of a disagreement between the two houses, as he thinks proper, but not beyond the day of the next stated session. He may from time to time, gives information concerning the state of government to the General Assembly, and recommends to their consideration such measures as he deems expedient. He has the power to grant reprieve after conviction, in all cases except those of impeachment.

Each bill which has passed both houses of the General Assembly is presented to the Governor in as timely a fashion as possible. If the Governor approves, he signs the bill and transmits it to the Secretary of the State. If he disapproves of it entirely, or of any section, the Secretary returns the disapproved bill or section for reconsideration to the House in which it originated. The General Assembly will either rewrite the bill to the satisfaction of the Governor, or by a roll call vote of two-thirds vote of both houses, may have it enacted into law if after five calendar days the Governor does not sign it.

The Governor has the authority to establish and oversee a Committee on Political Ideas (COPI), solely, or in delegation to or in conjunction with the initiative of the Senate, which also has sole initiative power. Its purpose is to be sure all ideas for political debate are discussed in a public and open-ended fashion. COPI has no lawmaking power, but serves as a resource for lawmakers. On a given topic, COPI receives applications from partisans, prioritizes their testimonies, and works through them until all ideas have been fully and publically aired. Written presentations for COPI are a maximum 2,000 words, presented orally, there is no limit on annotation and attachments, and are followed by open-ended dialogue in all directions until the partisan is satisfied that he has been fully heard.

Section 4:3: The Lieutenant Governor is a full-time position, and by virtue of his office is the President of the Senate, and while in committee of the whole may debate, and if the Senate is equally divided, cast the deciding vote.

In the event of the death, resignation, refusal to serve or removal from office of the Governor, the Lieutenant Governor will, upon taking the oath of office, serve as Governor until another is chosen at the next regular election for Governor and is duly qualified. In the event of the impeachment of the Governor or of his absence from the state, the Lieutenant Governor exercises the powers and duties of his office until his acquittal of impeachment charges or return from his absence, and serves as acting Governor until the Governor transmits to the Lieutenant Governor a written declaration that he is unable to exercise the duties of his office.

Absent the Governor's cooperation in such matters, the General Assembly will convene as soon as possible, and by a two-thirds vote may install the Lieutenant Governor as acting Governor. The Supreme Court has original and sole jurisdiction to adjudicate if the General Assembly cannot decide the matter itself. If the Lieutenant Governor becomes Governor, the President pro tempore of the Senate assumes the office of Lieutenant Governor. If this happens when the General Assembly is not in session, the Secretary of State convenes the General Assembly within 15 days to elect a new President pro tempore.

143

If the Governor-elect through death or due to other variables becomes unqualified to assume office, the Lieutenant Governor-elect assumes the office of Governor. The General Assembly, by two-thirds vote, has the power to make law to specify another manner for qualifying the replacement of the Governor-elect, or other succession needs as they arise.

Section 4:4: The Treasurer is a full-time position, and receives all monies belonging to the state, and disburses them only as directed by law. He pays no warrant, or order for the disbursement of public money, until the same has been registered in the office of the Comptroller. He oversees all matters of his office, is authorized to enter into contractual agreements as necessary and proper to conduct the state's business, and to issue bonds as directed by the Governor, subject to a majority vote of the General Assembly. He appoints a deputy to assist in all matters, and in seasons of need due to incapacity, the deputy will assume the Treasurer's office, or as necessary, for the duration of the term. The Treasurer will appoint a chief investment officer for investment of state funds. The General Assembly establishes an Investment Advisory Council to serve the Treasurer and the chief investment officer, and define the necessary criteria for sound investment policies.

The Treasurer publishes a statement of all receipts, payments, funds and debts of the state is published as the public desires or as prescribed by law, and is accessible on the state's website at all times as concurrently as practicable. He issues a complete annual statement, in print and on his website, in summary with all details, and an audited financial statement to the Governor, for the fiscal year ending September 30, and presented on or before October 15 of each year.

Section 4:5: The Secretary of State is a full-time position, and he oversees all matters of his office, is responsible for receiving from the local municipalities, and presenting to the General Assembly, an orderly and true tally for the election of all members of the General Assembly and Constitutional State Officers, and likewise for the United States Congress, no later than fifteen days after the election. He appoints a deputy to assist in all matters, and in seasons of need due to incapacity, the deputy assumes the Secretary's office, or as necessary, for the duration of the term.

The Secretary of State publishes an annual record of all state, county and town or city officers, elected and appointed, and all public facilities and properties belonging to the state. The Secretary of State appoints notaries public, sets their qualifications, issues certificates to those who qualify, and defines their terms of service. He has the safe keeping and custody of the

144

public records and documents, and particularly of the acts, resolutions and orders of the General Assembly, and record of the same. He performs all such duties as prescribed by law, and is keeper of the seal of the state, which will not be altered. The Secretary, in taking any action that is properly in the public domain, but not disclosed, is subject to reprimand or removal by the General Assembly.

The historic official arms, the great seal and the state flag, as recorded by the Secretary in the annual record, contains the state motto: QUI TRANSTULIT SUSTINET; and likewise, the Secretary of State records the historic state flower as the mountain laurel, the state bird as the American robin, the state animal as the sperm whale, the state insect as the praying mantis, the state shellfish as the Eastern oyster, the state fish as the American shad, the state tree as the white oak, the state name as the Constitution State, the state mineral as the garnet, the state song as Yankee Doodle, the state hero and heroine as Nathan Hale and Prudence Crandall, the state fossil as the dinosaur footprints of Eubrontes, the state folk dance as the square dance, the state cantata as Nutmeg, the state flagship and tall ship ambassador as the Freedom Schooner Amistad; and the historic state tartan; and a state poet laureate, state troubadour, the Charles Edward Ives Memorial Composer Laureate, may be appointed at the pleasure of the Secretary.

Section 4:6: The Comptroller is a full-time position, and he oversees all matters of his office. He adjusts and settles all public accounts and demands, except grants and orders of the General Assembly. He prescribes the mode of keeping and rendering all public accounts, and ex officio serves as one of the auditors of the accounts of the Treasurer. The General Assembly may assign him and the Treasurer other duties as they see fit. He appoints a deputy to assist in all matters, and in seasons of need due to incapacity, the deputy will assume the Comptroller's office, or as necessary, for the duration of the term.

Section 4:7: The Attorney General is a full-time position, and he oversees all matters of the criminal justice division. He has supervision over all legal matters in which the state is an interested party, and represents members of the General Assembly, Executive and Judiciary in the same, except where he himself requires recusal due to personal conflict, at which point the chief state's attorney represents him.

The Attorney General appoints a deputy to assist in all matters, and in seasons of need due to incapacity, the deputy will assume the Attorney General's office, or as necessary, for the duration of the term. The Attorney

General may appoint up to four associate attorneys general who will serve at his pleasure.

The criminal justice division is in charge of the investigation and prosecution of all criminal matters. The administrative head is the chief state's attorney for the whole state, nominated by the Attorney General and subject to ratification by the Senate. State's attorneys head each judicial district as established by law, with prosecutorial power devolving in the same order. The appointment of state's attorneys, and other attorneys as prescribed by law, is the responsibility of a commission composed of the chief state's attorney, and six members appointed by the governor and confirmed by the General Assembly, two of whom serve as judges of the Superior Court.

Section 4:8: Apart from the Governor and Lieutenant Governor, members of the Executive are to be electors of at least twenty-one years of age, their salary and expenses are determined by law, can only be changed for a time following the next election, and no member of the Executive is at the same time to hold any other position in local, state or federal government.

Article V
The Judicial

Section 5:1: The judicial power of the state is vested in the Supreme Court, an Appellate Court, a Superior Court, Probate Courts, Common Courts and other lower courts as the General Assembly will, from time to time, ordain and establish. The powers and jurisdiction of these courts are established by law. Member of the Supreme Court are full-time, and appointed judges of the lower courts are full-time or part-time at the discretion of the Supreme Court.

Section 5:2: Judges of all courts, except in those courts where judges are elected, are nominated by the Governor from candidates submitted by the judicial selection commission nominated by the Governor and approved by the Senate, which seeks qualified candidates in such numbers as prescribed by law. Judges so nominated are appointed by the General Assembly as the law prescribes, hold their offices for eight years, and may be removed by impeachment, by the Governor on the address of two-thirds of the General Assembly, or at the prerogative of the Supreme Court as prescribed by law. The General Assembly may also censure or suspend such judges for up to one year as the law prescribes.

Section 5:3: Judges of the lower courts are nominated by the Governor and appointed by the General Assembly as the law prescribes, and hold their offices for four years. Judges of probate are elected in their respective districts on the first Tuesday following the first Monday of November, 2010, and every four years thereafter.

Section 5:4: In the Common Courts, power is vested in committees of common judges. There are seven members in each committee, elected by the local municipalities annually, with as many such committees as each municipality sees fit, and with rules of procedure set by the same. These committees have the power, in non-felonious matters, and upon the written consent of all parties to a given complaint, to resolve issues so that they need not go through the regular court system. The location for the complaint is the town or city of the defendant's residency or business, and for defendants who live and work outside the state, the location reverts to the town or city of the plaintiff's residence or business. The committees of common judges guarantee a public hearing and resolution within six weeks of filing, with all decisions being final, and with no appeals in the regular courts unless otherwise stipulated in law.

Section 5:5: A statewide Common Court board exists to settle issues between the local Common Courts, including jurisdictional issues and concerns for mutual cooperation, and consists of thirteen members elected annually by the Common Court members, and sets its own protocol.

Section 5:6: The General Assembly is responsible for setting up an orderly court system under the auspices of the Judicial Department, defining the responsibilities and purview of each court, in all matters criminal and civil, and where resolution of all conflicts are dealt with most simply and speedily. The Chief Justice of the Supreme Court is head of the Judicial Department, and appoints a chief court administrator who serves at his pleasure, setting appropriate fees for service. All contracts with public or private concerns are made in open meetings, including all bidding processes, and with full access to the media.

Section 5:7: In all other courts, all cases must be brought to public trial in no more than twelve weeks from the original filing date, apart from a directive from the General Assembly in time of special reason for a specific case or set of cases. All pre-trial motions and the trial itself must be done in person before the judge or his appointed deputy.

Section 5:8: The Supreme Court meets in Hartford, holds final and conclusive jurisdiction for all legal disputes under state law, and is responsible for the State Library.

Section 5:9: Probate courts are established covering local districts throughout the states as determined by the General Assembly, and probate judges are elected every four years in the districts they are to serve.

Section 5:10: The Superior Court is coextensive throughout the state, headquartered in Hartford, with branches as established by the General Assembly. It is the sole court of original jurisdiction apart from matters where the probate courts has jurisdiction, and has authority over small claims and the juvenile court system. The Appellate Court is coextensive throughout the state, located alongside the Superior Court.

Section 5:11: The Judicial Selection Committee comprises twelve members representing the interests of the whole state as defined by the General Assembly, as nominated by the Governor, for service in the Superior, Appellate and Supreme Courts. Such appointed judges are subject to recall on terms defined by the General Assembly.

Section 5:12: The qualifications for attorneys to serve in the courts are set by the General Assembly, and likewise for jurors. The court system is easily accessible for those filing claims pro se, and also provides public defenders for those who cannot afford an attorney.

Section 5:13: Any person is free to grant the power of attorney to one or several other persons to act legally on his behalf, for seasons and purposes clearly delineated in all necessary detail, congruent with choosing an open or closed contract. In civil legal proceedings, plaintiffs bear court costs when the defendant is proven innocent. An out of court settlement is always available until the moment the case reaches trial.

Article VI
Electors

Section 6:1: Every U.S. citizen of at least eighteen years in age, being a bona fide resident of a Connecticut town or city, and upon taking such oath, is qualified to be an elector as prescribed by law. He is able to pre-register up to six months prior to his eighteenth birthday, and is eligible to hold public office unless the given office specifies otherwise.

Section 6:2: The General Assembly, as prescribed by law, determines the offenses and convictions by which the right to be and privileges of an elector are forfeit, and how the same may be restored. The General Assembly makes law to support the privilege of free suffrage, prescribing the manner of regulating and conducting meetings of the electors, and prohibits under due penalty any undue influence from power, bribery, tumult and other improper conduct.

Section 6:3: The right to secrecy in the casting of votes in inviolate, all votes of the electors for any public office are by ballot, whether in print, by mechanical device or computerized system, and no such device or system can be used for the purpose of a straight party line vote.

Section 6:4: At the elections for any public office or in any related civil process, the electors are privileged from arrest during their attendance upon, and in going to and returning from the same. At the elections for any public office or ballot question, the General Assembly may, as prescribed by law, provide electors opportunity to vote by absentee ballot if their access to the polling place is restricted due to illness, job or school requirements, physical disability, or religious tenet regarding the day of the week.

Section 6:5: The citizens of the state have the right to petition the Legislature for any question to be placed on the next biennial ballot, for specified legal or non-binding purpose. The question a) is no more than thirty words total, b) is signed by at least 100,000 duly registered voters on sheets designating the local municipality in which the citizen claims to hold current registration, c) signatures are submitted to the municipal registrars for validation no later than July 1, forwarded to the Secretary of State no later than August 1 with a tally of valid signatures, so that an accurate aggregate may be known, and d) it contemplates specific action by the Legislature. If it is a legal matter, the Legislature is bound to adopt it as law if voted on by a majority of electors. If it is a non-binding matter, and voted on by a majority of electors, the Legislature is to openly debate its import for possible action.

Article VII
Elections

Section 7:1: The residency of electors is first determined, and then annually recertified, by local municipalities, and residency must be certified no less than two weeks before participation in any election. When an elector's status is in dispute, the matter is resolved by the plaintiff making his case before the Common Court, and if he is unsatisfied, before the Common Court statewide board. To challenge the decision of the statewide board, the plaintiff must start again with the local Common Court, offering new evidence.

Section 7:2: All electors, upon initial certification within a given municipality, will take the following oath: "I solemnly swear (or affirm), that as a legal citizen of the United States, and resident of [name of municipality], I agree to abide by the Constitution of the United States and the Constitution of the State of Connecticut, so help me God" (this last clause being optional). At the time of voting, all electors must show a state issued photo identification card and/or other such proof of identity as determined by law.

Section 7:3: Local municipalities offer the option of mail-in ballots for statewide elections to those who apply and give reason for their absence from the state on election day, the ballots are mailed to the elector no sooner than thirty days before such an election, and the returned ballots must be postmarked no later than election day at 5:00 p.m.

Section 7:4: All means of tabulating votes must be via optical scan of paper ballots, and are subject to safeguards to maintain the anonymity of all votes cast. For electors who have disability in reading, understanding or casting their votes, the local municipality provides assistance, and in a way where the anonymity of the vote cast is maintained.

Section 7:5: All municipalities provide the Secretary of State their annual voter registration list by October 15 each year, making any necessary emendations as needed up to two weeks before a statewide election, and these lists are to comport to a uniform system as directed by the Secretary of State. All convicted and/or incarcerated felons, whether in state or federal court, forfeit their voting rights, and restoration of voting rights may occur by petition to the Common Court five years after the penalty and/or sentence is completed.

Section 7:6: Political parties may be formed by at least ten citizens, submitting paperwork as determined by the Secretary of State, and with party names that are readily distinct from other recognized parties. For a political party to be recognized on a statewide ballot, such a party must have a) secured at least three percent of the vote by its leading vote getter in the prior election, or b) upon the petition of at least ten thousand electors ninety days prior to the given election.

Section 7:7: Primary elections are held whenever a recognized political party has at least two candidates for the same office, where each received at least fifteen percent of the vote in a duly recognized and open party convention vote. Only registered members of a political party may vote in their party's primary, the names of party nominees will be transmitted to the Secretary of State in a timely fashion, and primaries are held on the third Tuesday of May of the election year.

Section 7:8: Each ballot in any election clearly identifies all candidates by the office they seek, their party affiliation, or as an independent. The order in which the candidate names appear will be determined by a random process each election, and will be uniform on all ballots once determined.

Section 7:9: For any candidate wishing to be placed on a municipal or state ballot, having failed to secure a party nomination, he must collect the signatures of at least five percent of duly registered voters in the district, and submit those signatures no less than 120 days before the election. Candidates for a write-in ballot, whether initiated by self or a drafting group, must be clear in the singular identity of the candidate, and filed with the local municipality for local elections, and with the Secretary of State for state government offices, no later than fifteen days prior to the election.

Section 7:10: The security necessary to ensure fair, accessible and honest elections is the responsibility of the local municipality, insofar as there is no conflict with state or federal law. Local municipalities establish the protocol for the presence of poll watchers from recognized political parties and others so interested. No partisan politicking, in any form, may occur within 100 feet of a polling place on election day.

Section 7:11: All municipalities submit the results of an election to the office of the Secretary of State within 24 hours of the polls closing, according to protocol set by the Secretary of State; and upon petition to the Secretary, may be granted further time if discrepancies remain. Uniform standards for the hours the polls are open are set by the Secretary of State.

Section 7:12: Any elector who believes another person is guilty of deliberate interference in an honest and free election, will submit his evidence in person to the Common Court, and the accused will give answer. If the accused is found suspect, he will then appear likewise before the Common Court statewide board, if found suspect again, the matter becomes a legal one for the regular courts, and its nature is that of a felony. Vacancies in any state or federal office, unless otherwise defined, will be filled by a special election within ninety days.

Section 7:13: Challenges to any election returns must be mounted a) by the losing candidate, or b) by certified petition of at least fifteen percent of the electors of the affected district within thirty days, and only in cases where the official vote tally shows a margin of victory of no more than one percent, and then a complete re-canvass will be ordered. If ultimately there is a tie vote, the winner will be determined by a public coin toss.

Section 7:14: All ballots in state elections are to be maintained in the archives of the Secretary of State for at least ten years, open to inspection, and likewise in municipal archives for local elections.

Section 7:15: In each U.S. Presidential election year, a statewide primary is to be held on the first Tuesday in March, with oversight conducted by the local municipalities, and results transmitted to the Secretary of State within 24 hours unless petitioned otherwise.

Section 7:16: Monies donated to a political candidate's committee is an expression of free speech, and there is no limit, except that all donors must be U.S. citizens. No money may be solicited by the candidate or advocacy group before the campaign officially begins. All monies received are published daily on the candidate's website, with the names, amount and postal addresses of the donor. If any elector believes that the solicitation of funds for the actual campaign has been illicit, he may petition the Common Court to have the candidate or advocacy group to answer any questions, with specificity. Deliberate election fraud is a felony, and all fraudulent funds go into the state treasury.

Article VIII
Amendments to the Constitution

Section 8:1: An amendment to the Constitution may be proposed by any member of the General Assembly, and upon the roll call vote affirmation of three-fourths of its members, takes effect. If the vote for such an amendment is greater than a majority but less than three-fourths, the question is then submitted to all the electors at the next general election, and if affirmed by a majority, takes effect.

Section 8:2: The General Assembly, upon the roll call vote and affirmation of two-thirds of its members, may provide for the convening of a Constitutional Convention to amend or revise the Constitution of the state, but not earlier than ten years from the date of convening any prior convention, and the convention will convene within the next twelve months.

Section 8:3: If twenty years have elapsed since the prior Constitutional Convention, the option is to be placed before all electors of the state at the next general election, "Shall there be a Constitutional Convention to amend or revise the Constitution of the State." If a majority of the electors say yes, the convention will convene within twelve months.

Section 8:4: Proposals made at the Constitutional Convention, to amend it in part or revise it in the whole, are submitted to the electors not later than two months subsequent to the adjournment of the convention. It takes effect if approved by a majority of the electors, within thirty days or as otherwise specified by the proposal of the convention.

Article IX
General Laws

Section 9:1: The General Laws, in applying the purposes of the State Constitution, are by definition general, written as minimally yet comprehensively as possible, leaving the necessary and more substantial, yet simply defined specifics, to the state offices and departments responsible for particular oversight and enforcement. Any claims against the state are resolved in manners prescribed by law.

Section 9:2: All terms used in the Constitution and General Laws, and their applicability, are understood according to the plain meaning of normal English usage and specific context. If there is a disagreement between parties concerning the definition and applicability of a particular term, it is to be resolved ahead of usage, in a) Common Court; b) Superior Court; or c) legislative debate. All use of the male pronoun is assumed, congruent with normal English usage, to be gender inclusive unless otherwise delineated.

Section 9:3: Those under the age of eighteen years are of minority age, as of the eighteenth year, the person reaches majority age for all legal matters unless otherwise stipulated.

Section 9:4: Any person who knowingly provides false information on any document he or she signs, in private contracts or in government business, is liable for immediate loss of related privilege, and for penalties as assessed in Common Court or Superior Court. Any person who deliberately subverts public order in any capacity is guilty of a felony.

Section 9:5: Privacy rights exist where a) the substance is original with the person and does not interfere with the life, liberty or property of others, b) protection for the innocent in criminal matters, and c) when state or national defense against enemies without or within is needful, as accountable to the Legislature and courts.

Section 9:6: Legal holidays, where all public institutions are closed except for emergency personnel, include: New Year's Day (January 1); Martin Luther King Day (the first Monday on or after January 15); President's Day (the third Monday in February); Memorial Day (the last Monday in May); Independence Day (July 4); Labor Day (the first Monday in September); Columbus Day (the second Monday in October); Veterans Day (November 11); Thanksgiving Day (the fourth Thursday of November); and Christmas Day (December 25). The Governor may also issue a call for a special holiday, and as approved by the Legislature.

Section 9:7: If any private or governmental contractual obligation or constitutional requirement falls on a Sunday or a legal holiday, or religiously required holiday, the next day or next business day suffices as the deadline; if any legal holiday falls on Saturday, the preceding Friday will be the day; if any legal holiday falls on a Sunday, the subsequent Monday will be the day.

Section 9:8: The standard time for the state equals the seventy-fifth meridian west of Greenwich; it is modified at 2:00 a.m. in advance by one hour on the second Sunday in March, until 2:00 a.m. on the first Sunday of November.

Section 9:9: All members of the state and municipal government, for each term in service, and those in sworn service to a government function, for the given specific term, will make a public oath orally, or alternatively if need be due to prohibitive exigency, in written form. Oaths will be administered by the most senior government official available in the given context.

Section 9:10: The oath spoken is this: "I solemnly swear (or affirm), in service to the Constitution of the United States and the Constitution of the State of Connecticut, in all honesty and faithfulness, and to the best of my abilities, to discharge all my assigned responsibilities with impartiality, so help me God" (this last clause being optional).

Section 9:11: All legal promises made in any context of government service or private contract are fully enforceable upon the signatures of two parties with the signature of a third witness, which may or may not be a notary public; or in the event of three or more parties making a legal agreement, their number is sufficient.

Section 9:12: There are three types of legal contracts for all business transactions, in government and the private sector – two forms of "open contract" and one form of a "closed contract." An open contract must be on one side of a common 8x11 piece of paper, and if "simple," it has a maximum of fifty words in the body of the text; if "regular," it has a maximum of 300 words in the body of the text; a closed contract is not thus limited. At the top of all contracts the following disclosure is required, and to be immediately signed and dated underneath by the agreeing parties: "This contract is either a simple open contract [ ], a regular open contract [ ] or a closed contract [ ], according to the laws of Connecticut – check only one box to the right." When advertising any product or service to the public requiring the signing of a contract, it must be likewise stated clearly in normal speech, or printed clearly that such a contract is either a simple or regular open contract, or a closed contract according to Connecticut law. All disputes concerning open contracts are adjudicated only in the Common Courts.

Section 9:13: Along with detailed and current information provided on the state's website relative to their public functions, the personal websites of all public officials must provide full transparency as to the interface of their public and private interests, in both cases with simple access. They are free to conduct business, relative to which their participation in public life grants them no special benefit, unless otherwise stipulated by law. Where a conflict of interest may arise, the public official is to disclose all such concerns in specificity, so that the people may monitor such potential cause for conflict. If the public official is charged with and found guilty of using his office for special benefit and/or personal gain, it is a felony, and he will be liable for immediate removal from office, a minimum ten-year ban from subsequent public office, a minimum of treble monetary damages, payable as the courts may decide, and other penalties as the courts may decide, and for which the Common Courts cannot adjudicate. The same rules apply when the public official leaves office relative to his time of service.

Section 9:14: All candidates for public office must maintain an official campaign website; they are to disclose donor names with current postal addresses, with amount given within, immediately. There is no limit to monies that can be given, and all such candidates are bound by Section 5:1 and its enforcements insofar as their campaigns may neither promise nor solicit special benefit. Monies are donated to a political committee set up by the candidate or advocacy group when the campaign officially begins. If any elector believes that the solicitation of funds for the actual campaign began before the campaign committee was formed, he may petition the Common Court to have the candidate or advocacy group to answer any questions, with specificity. Willful deceit on the candidates part is a felony.

Section 9:15: All citizens are free to lobby public officials as individuals or as groups, for matters in which they have interest, spending monies as necessary; they are accountable to the legal scrutiny of any elector, group of electors or public officials, if evidence is presented in court that they have engaged in promise or delivery of goods or services that constitute special benefit, and they are thus held liable if convicted.

Section 9:16: All meetings by government agencies and/or public officials are public by definition, open to all, excepting discussion of constitutional privacy matters, and accountable to public inquiry and commentary. They are announced with ample advance notice on appropriate websites and by other means, apart from emergency meetings voted on by the General Assembly.

Section 9:17: All public meetings may be fully recorded in any fashion, given reasonable accommodation, communications among public officials are fully available to any elector in any medium recorded by the public officials, as soon as practicable.

Section 9:18: Taxes for the operation of state government are collected only by means of a) a state sales tax, and b) fees for service as approved by the General Assembly. The sales tax is uniform and collected only on goods sold in the state, or leases other than for primary residence; and is reported and paid by businesses on a weekly basis, or by individuals on a monthly basis. Exempted goods are primary personal needs in matters of rent, food, clothing and medicine. The percentage figure for the state sales tax is determined by the General Assembly in due proportion each year relative to budgetary needs, after the budget is passed. The only organizations free from liability for the sales tax are those recognized in prevailing law by the federal Internal Revenue Service as 501(c)3 and 501(c)4 organizations. Any person charged with and convicted of deliberate tax fraud is guilty of a felony.

Section 9:19: If revenues exceed the budget by up to twenty percent, those monies are to be set aside in a publicly viewable bank account for emergency use as determined by a two-thirds vote of each House of the General Assembly, returnable to the general budget relative to subsequent revenue deficits that may occur within the fiscal year. For revenues that exceed the twenty percent overage, they are to be set aside in another publicly viewable bank account, to be applied to the subsequent year's budget before the tax percentage for that year is calculated.

Section 9:20: The General Assembly only proposes and enacts legislation for the state as a whole, with all powers delegated to it by the citizens through their local municipalities. All bills for expenditure of funds originate in the House, confirmation of appointed officers and judges lies in the Senate, and a conference committee may be appointed by both the Senate and House to reconcile the language of final bills to be submitted to the Governor.

Section 9:21: There is an office for the State Capitol Police on the Capitol grounds to maintain order, each officer is a member of a duly sworn local police department, and the jurisdiction of the Capitol Police officers is trans-local in accord with their assignments.

Section 9:22: Members of federally recognized Indian tribes resident in Connecticut are full citizens of the state, those living on Indian lands have the privileges extended to them per federal law, and may enter into mutual compacts and contracts with state and municipal governments. Monies received by casinos operating on federally recognized Indian reservations are at their discretion, along with other revenues generated, so long as there is no violation of federal and state civil rights. The Department of Revenue has the power to make laws to control traffic access from the state into and out of Indian reservations, in cooperation with overlapping federal jurisdictions, assessing tolls as deemed necessary for the well being of the state.

Article X
State Departments

Section 10:1: Each state department has a Secretary as head, appointed by the Governor, subject to approval by a three-quarters vote of the General Assembly, sets directives consistent with the Constitution and oversight of the General Assembly, maintains a current website, and they serve respectively as executive officers. Each Secretary appoints a deputy to assist in all matters, and in seasons of need due to incapacity, the deputy will assume the Secretary's office, or as necessary, for the duration of the term.

Section 10:2: If any Secretary any action that is properly in the public domain but done without due transparency, he is subject to reprimand or removal by a three-quarters vote of the General Assembly. When a department head cannot continue to serve, temporarily or permanently, the

Governor will appoint an acting head, and nominate a new head within thirty days.

Section 10:3: Each department has its own budget, and is responsible for setting any and all appropriate fees for service, subject to approval by the General Assembly. All contracts with public or private concerns are made in open meetings, including all bidding processes, and with full access to the media.

Section 10:4: Whenever policy by means of writing directives is to be debated and decided, it occurs in public meetings of the department. All itemized directives must be in clear language of 100 words or less; unless permitted by a vote of two-thirds of the General Assembly.

Section 10:5: The Department of Administration has a Secretary as its head who is responsible for all aspects of oversight concerning staff planning, budgeting and necessary coordination for all departments of state government; and for administering all aspects of personnel policy and material provisions for all departments.

The Secretary maintains the state's website, concurrently on all matters of the people's trust, linking all constitutional officer and state department websites, and also the individual and/or official websites of all elected and appointed members of government.

Section 10:6: The Department of Revenue has a Secretary as its head who is responsible for all aspects of oversight in order to secure the orderly collection of taxes and fees as authorized by the General Assembly, including authority to negotiate with other States on interface with their tax systems.

Section 10:7: The Department of Business and Labor has a Secretary as its head who is responsible for all aspects in oversight of the coordination of all business relationships between the state, other states, the federal government, organized labor and private entities. He always preferring to contract with businesses headquartered or located in the state if skill, quality and cost are competitive; all state contracts are open contracts unless the General Assembly makes exception by a two-thirds vote, to then be entered as a specific rule with the Department.

The Secretary sets standards for public and private corporations or associations doing business in the state, including truth in advertising, all professional and occupational licensing standards for respective private accrediting agencies, within and without the state, lacking such, the General Assembly may create their own, and determines to whom to issues licenses for doing business in the state, and the procedure for application.

The Secretary oversees the rights of organized labor, including transparency in accountability to its members and the right to secret ballot in all elections, and no person can be compelled to work on a day he announces ahead of time as his religiously defined weekly day of rest. The Secretary sets standards for indemnified insurance companies, services and products, and the people have the right to organize an alternative cooperative plan where liability is shared, but ultimately the responsibility belongs to each individual or corporate owner. The Department of Business and Labor sets standards for any private betting concerns in the state, apart from Indian casinos; all such betting concerns must use open contracts.

Section 10:8: The Department of Banking has a Secretary as its head who is responsible for all aspects in oversight of licensing, transparency and standards regarding the integrity of banks and credit unions doing business in the state, standards for stocks and bonds, credit reporting agencies, sales of financial products and services, all being consistent with a transparently open and free market economy.

Section 10:9: The Department of Public Safety has a Secretary as its head who is responsible for all aspects in oversight of safety standards for the maximum and equal protection of life and property of all people within the state, all state departments and municipalities are subject to their standards unless otherwise stipulated by law, and all in service to a statewide uniform code.

The Secretary oversees the state police, uniform standards for fire safety supervised by a state fire marshal, the 911 emergency phone system, standards for private detectives and private security guards, use of firearms, a uniform state building and demolition code, machinery operations, a uniform standard for working conditions, limits on contractually compulsory work hours, animal control and well being, and for working with municipalities, other states and federal law enforcement where needful.

Section 10:10: The Department of Public Health has a Secretary as its head who is responsible for all aspects of oversight in the prevention of communicable diseases and other threats to public health, oversees the Connecticut Blood Bank, working with state and private hospitals to ensure the most adequate possible supply. All state departments and municipalities are subject to the Department's standards unless otherwise stipulated by law, all in service to a statewide uniform code, and maintains all vital statistics concerning public health.

The Secretary may not violate the religious or philosophic convictions of persons who may wish to opt out of certain standards, such as immunizations, so long as such persons can articulate before the Common Court their reasons and rationale for the best well being of those under their charge; if not satisfied with a Common Court ruling, they may appeal to Superior Court.

The Governor appoints an Independent Advisory Board of twelve members, all experts in public health matters, subject to the approval of the General Assembly, to advise the Secretary of the Department of Public Health.

The legal age for the purchase and public use of alcoholic beverages is 21. Insofar as consistent with prevailing federal law, those who abuse themselves by means of alcohol, nicotine, other controlled substances or illegal substances, and do not harm the life, liberty or property of another person, pay the penalty in their own persons, and are not to be penalized more than for a misdemeanor, also having no legal right to impose themselves upon others for remedy, but private agencies dedicated to charity on their behalf may offer such help.

Insofar as consistent with prevailing federal law, illegal sale of alcohol, controlled substances, and sale of illegal substances, where there is no resulting deprivation of life, liberty or property caused any other person, does not merit incarceration; only fines as determined by the General Assembly, and/or suspension of driver's license; special laws may be crafted to penalize those who sell to or supply minors.

At the beginning of life, insofar as consistent with federal law, human abortion may only be performed by a licensed physician in a hospital when otherwise the mother would die. At the end of life, the power of attorney may be exercised in writing ahead of time, or in the witness of at least three people present, who sign affidavits accordingly, so as to effect the refusal by the patient of any extraordinary means to prolong life; the supply of water and nutrition insofar as possible, is ordinary.

All food, medicine and clothing sold in Connecticut, regardless of origin, will carry a simple, prominent and easy to read label, with the applicable category or categories being checked off: all natural [ ]; natural with some synthetic additions [ ]; synthetic with some natural elements [ ]; all synthetic [ ]; contains genetically modified organisms (GMOs). All ingredients are likewise to be listed in a suitable place, with clear and simple delineation of benefits and risks for food, food supplements, medicine and GMOs.

Section 10:11: The Department of Public Utilities has a Secretary as its head who is responsible for all aspects of oversight in coordinating all utilities in service to reliable access by the public. The Secretary oversees utilities and energy sources made available for the public use, for the well being, safety, environmental and economic health of the state, including telecommunications, internet access, electricity generation, nuclear energy, natural gas, fuel oil, renewable energy, and other sources, as produced by private companies in a free market economy with all property rights protected. The Secretary oversees licenses, standards safety, along with coordination between municipalities; and all such companies will provide their services only by means of open contracts.

Section 10:12: The Department of Public Works has a Secretary as its head who is responsible for all aspects in oversight of planning, construction and maintenance of capital projects and real property under state jurisdiction.

Section 10:13: The Department of Transportation has a Secretary as its head who is responsible for all aspects in oversight of transportation infrastructure under state jurisdiction, including ground, air and water, in concert with federal authority where applicable; with the highest safety and orderly flow on all state highways and bridges being the premier concern, and for mass transit programs involving multiple municipalities, whether under private or state jurisdiction.

The Governor appoints a harbor master for all harbors on Long Island Sound, under whom deputy harbor masters may be appointed, to oversee the safety of all navigation, anchoring, docking, sewage, transport of goods, and licensure for all ships and pilots. Penalties for operating aircraft or machine powered watercraft under the influence of alcohol or other judgment impairing substances are the same as in Section 27:7.

Section 10:14: The Department of Social Services has a Secretary as its head who is responsible for all aspects of oversight for organizing state resources as a means of last resort, in times of social need, for any person whose family structures, private or municipal resources have proven insufficient, thus threatening their lives, liberties or properties, and to work with other states as necessary, where in all cases, private resources offered are to be utilized first.

With every annual election of Common Court members, the Common Court statewide board will poll all such members for the twelve most highly regarded members to also serve as an Independent Advisory Committee to the Department of Social Services, and this Committee will have privileged access to all necessarily private records in the Department of Social Services.

For children whose safety and well being are thus endangered, the Department of Social Services may set up a system of orphanages, group homes or host homes to meet all the provisional, physical health and mental health, safety, social and educational needs of such children.

The Secretary works with private adoption agencies, as approved by the municipality in which they are located, to assure the best possible placement of children eligible for adoption, consistent with the wishes of the responsible parents or legal guardians, as reviewed by the Independent Advisory Committee, with the priority of locating married households as adoptive homes. The priority for the caring of displaced children, or those eligible for adoption, is always to keep children in the state, but as a last resort, the Secretary may negotiate with other states to meet these needs, and reciprocally as need be.

Section 10:15: The Department of Land and Water Use has a Secretary as its head who is responsible for all aspects in oversight of all state lands and waters, historical sites, cultural centers and parks, for public access, safety and enjoyment, and for coordinating municipalities and private enterprise where requested, in service to the healthiest possible balance between settled and unsettled lands where state forestation and open space is a discrete benefit, and for the maximum possible agricultural use as well.

Section 10:16: The Department of Environment has a Secretary as its head who is responsible for all aspects of oversight for the best possible sustainable health and cleanliness of air, water and land in the state, for the benefit of all persons in all their sensory perceptions; in concert as needful with bilateral arrangements with other states, and with federal policies among the states.

Section 10:17: The Department of Motor Vehicles has a Secretary as its head who is responsible for all aspects of oversight for motor vehicle and driver licensing. The Department issues photo-identification cards for drivers and non-drivers, required of all residents of majority age, where the applicant needs to provide his verifiable birth certificate, and all other residential and contact information as required.

Provisional driver's licenses are issued to applicants of at least seventeen years of age, with restrictions determined by the Department. If there are no tickets issued by any municipal or state police officer for driving offenses for the first year after receiving the provisional license, then at that time a permanent driver's license is issued. If there is one offense, and in addition to any legal liability, then the provisional status remains until the driver is nineteen years old. If there are at least two offenses, and in addition to any legal liability, the provisional status remains until the driver is twenty years old. For three offenses, and in addition to any legal liability, the provisional status remains until the driver is twenty-one years old.

All motor vehicles principally garaged in the state are registered with the Department, and issued titles of ownership by the same. The Department oversees all issues of safety inspection and emissions standards, and the Secretary or designated official adjudicates any willful violation of safety standards in public hearings, with an appeals process in place.

The Department issues licenses and standards for driving schools, dealers, repairers, wreckers, towers, storage facilities and junk yards, and oversees safety rules for the sale, distribution and disposal of gasoline, diesel, oil and related fuels. All registered vehicles in the state require either a) legal indemnification for personal injury or death, and/or loss of property, by a registered insurance company within the state; or b) an alternative co-operative plan among drivers, where liability is shared, but ultimately the responsibility belongs to each individual or corporate owner.

All traffic laws in the state regarding issues of safety are uniform and set by the Secretary except where local distinctives are recognized. Safety standards are set by municipal, state and federal agencies responsible for the given road.

Anyone convicted of driving under the influence of alcohol or any other substance that impairs driving abilities, as defined by the Secretary, or of deliberately reckless driving, defined by the same, is liable the first time for a fine of no less than $10,000.00, the second time, a suspension of the driver's license for no less than one year with a new fine of no less than $20,000.00, and the third time it is a felony with additional fines, suspensions and jail time as determined by the regular courts.

Section 10:18: The Department of Education has a Secretary as its head who is responsible for all aspects in oversight of the University of Connecticut and its public university system, its academic standards, and in coordinating mutual efforts chosen by municipalities with respect to public primary and secondary education.

The state maintains a system of higher education including the University of Connecticut, dedicated to excellence in higher education where the spirit of academic freedom and liberal arts inquiry in service to unalienable rights is celebrated. The General Assembly is charged with its details and oversight.

The education of children is the primary freedom and responsibility of parents or legal guardians; the oversight of municipal public education in primary and secondary schools belongs to the local municipality, based on the residency requirements, standards and protocol it sets.

There will always be free public elementary and secondary schools in the state, rooted in the primary responsibility and liberty of the parents or legal guardians, and initiated and maintained by the local municipalities. The monies to pay for the education of all residential students of the municipality are to be collected from local taxes and fees voted on in the annual town meeting, are to be apportioned evenly on behalf of all registered school-age children, and at the discretion of their parents or legal guardians, these monies may be assigned to schools run by the municipality, privately run schools, or home schooled children. For the latter, they are entitled to access public education facilities and/or extra-curricular activities, subject to payment of an appropriate fee commensurate with the cost for municipal school students.

Academic standards are set by each school system, municipal, private or home schools.
Local municipalities may join with other municipalities to form regional schools as they see fit, and likewise work with the Secretary.

Section 10:19: The Department of Corrections has a Secretary as its head who is responsible for all aspects of oversight for administering the incarceration and remittance of those convicted of offenses under state jurisdiction, for their reintegration into society, working with municipalities as interested, and may enter into reciprocal compacts with other states for incarceration purposes, as deemed needful.

All inmates are to be separated according to sex, minority versus majority age, and levels of offense, so that no harm will come to any inmate. For the conviction of committing even one sex crime while in prison, the offender will be remanded to a segregated place that removes the possibility for another such crime for the balance of the sentence. No pornographic or other material that dehumanizes people or abuses animals is allowed, and the Secretary may set other standards in conjunction with the General Assembly.

Private chaplains are given appropriate access to minister to the needs of prisoners thus interested, and are accountable to affirm the constitutional unalienable rights for all people equally. For women who give birth while in prison, the Secretary will work with the Department of Social Services to define the best possible care for the children. Every municipality has its own jail, headed by the police department, and sets standards overseen by the Secretary. Regional and state correctional facilities are run by wardens appointed by the Secretary, subject to approval by the General Assembly.

Section 10:20: The Department of Emergency Management has a Secretary as its head who is responsible for all aspects of oversight in coordinating state resources in the event of an emergency declared by the Governor or the federal government, subject to the personal hands-on leadership of the Governor as needed. The Governor is the commander-in-chief of state defense, including the National Guard, the militia, and all state and municipal law enforcement agencies, and related support structures, to maintain safety and order in times of a declared state of emergency, and working in concert with the federal armed services as jurisdictional overlap dictates.

Section 10:21: The Department of Veterans has a Secretary as its head who is responsible for all aspects of oversight in coordinating state resources for the needs of all veterans of the U.S. Armed Services and the Connecticut National Guard when federal and private resources and structures are insufficient.

Section 10:22: The Department of Public Information has a Secretary as its head who is responsible for all aspects of oversight in the dissemination of all state information to the public, including the advancement of tourism.

Section 10:23: All those who work for the state are to be hired on no other basis but qualification to perform the job. They may choose, in legal terms, to be a sub-contractor or an employee, and in either case, by open contract, and are to be paid sufficiently well so as to purchase their own benefits, with total compensation being reasonably commensurate with the private sector, and subject to annual review.

Article XI
Marriage Law

Section 11:1: All persons hold the unalienable rights to life, liberty and property, and therefore they hold equal dignity and protection under due process of law. The historic family unit, rooted in the marriage of one man and one woman and the raising of children, is the basic institution in society. No punitive laws may exist to restrict private association, whether heterosexual or homosexual in nature, yet all persons are accountable for the public consequences of their private associations and actions, and they will in no way deprive others of life, liberty or property.

Section 11:2: Marriage covenants are publicly solemnized by members of the clergy, a justice of the peace or others as determined by the General Assembly, and registered in the local municipality where performed.

Section 11:3: No person may marry anyone closer than a third cousin, nor to an in-law to a valid marriage, nor to a member of a stepfamily, nor to a minor. Only heterosexual monogamous marriages from other states or nations are recognized.

Section 11:4: Divorce is only permitted in the case of infidelity, abandonment or abuse, and in all matters of family conflicts coming before the court, the well being of children is foremost.

Section 11:5: Fathers who do not wed the mothers of their children are fully liable for the financial provision for their children, and mothers who abandon their children likewise, with cognate concerns determined by the courts.

Article XII
Municipal Government

Section 12:1: All local municipalities have the prerogative of home rule in matters that concern them only, or those matters not otherwise delineated in state or federal law.

Section 12:2: There are eight historic counties in the state: Hartford, New Haven, New London, Fairfield, Windham, Litchfield, Middlesex and Tolland; and they are free to organize according to the intents of their constituent municipalities.

Section 12:3: All municipalities, as incorporated "towns," have annual town meetings, at the same time each year, announced at the conclusion of the prior year's annual meeting, then at appropriate pre-intervals with suitable details, on the towns' website, also by post to all town residents, and through other due means of publicity.

Section 12:4: All matters of local government not affected by state or federal law, and definitions and delegation of the people's authority for the common well being, is subject to a majority vote of all electors at town meeting. If any matter decided at the town meeting is unsatisfactory to the written and verified petitions of twenty percent of the town electors within thirty days, a special meeting will be called no later than another thirty days for a new vote on the disputed matter.

Section 12:5: All municipalities elect their own registrars for the keeping of the vital statistics of the state – certificates of local births, adoptions, marriage and deaths, and on all birth certificates, the names of both the biological father and mother are to be listed, in all adoption records, the same is likewise required, but may be withheld from public scrutiny until the adopted child reaches majority age.

Section 12:6: All municipalities elect their own clerk, who keeps the town seal unaltered, and oversees all transactions made in the name of the town.

Section 12:7: Municipalities alone have the right to assess local taxes for their needs, to set local fees as needful, oversee public libraries, subject to uniform standards set by the office of the Secretary of State and in conjunction with other municipalities. Municipalities alone have authority for zoning laws, and may cooperate with other municipalities where oversight is naturally shared, may likewise cooperate in other chosen endeavors, and disputes between municipalities are decided by the statewide Common Court board.

Section 12:8: Polling places are set by local municipalities, as are the voting districts within the given municipality, sheriffs and/or constables are elected or appointed at the discretion of the local municipalities, and coordinated by and accountable to uniform standards set by the office of the Attorney General.

Section 12:9: Local municipalities are responsible for maintaining a fund to help economically distressed or disabled residents in their midst, especially in matters of basic needs and safety within their homes, including uninterrupted essential utility service, and may also, as asked, coordinate private efforts for the welfare of needy residents, and also as a local last resort, appropriate funds for the same.

Chapter Ten
Simplified Federal Law

Based on the six pillars of honest politics as translated into appropriate context, the power of a level playing field, the power of checks and balances, and via the power of Occam's razor, here is a written proposal that simplifies the U.S. Constitution and greatly reduces the U.S. Code from 48,000 (as of 2006) to 25 pages (and serves the minimizing or abolition of the huge corpus of subsequent federal regulations, such as the 70,000 pages for the Internal Revenue Service (also, as of 2006), or nearly the same for business regulations, plus health care etc.). As with the simplifying of Connecticut law, the result can produce simplicity, truth telling and transparency in politics. And a template can be made available for any interested nation, as well as for their states or regions.

The Declaration of Independence is couched in the historical backdrop and language of a reluctant rebellion against tyrannical power, when genuine reformation of the relationship with Great Britain, rooted in English Common Law, would have been fully satisfactory. The thinking of the signatories was rooted in the Protestant Reformation that did not initially seek severance from the Roman Catholic Church, but only its reformation, and also more proximately rooted in the First Great Awakening.

But in both cases, war came nonetheless, spinning into gear following the words of Martin Luther at the Diet of Worms, "Here I stand ...", and with the opening words of the Declaration, "When in the course of human events ..." The right to sever political bonds is the predicate for the Declaration of Independence, and the right to abolish and rewrite federal and state constitutional law is likewise foundational – such rights uniquely stem the possibility of military wars. And the goal is always reformation and reconciliation, as we see in the uneven but increasingly healthy histories that followed in Roman Catholic and Protestant relations, and in British and American relations.

We have already noted the words of James Madison, "if the laws be so voluminous that they cannot be read, or so incoherent that they cannot be understood," then it does us little good to have an elected government. Madison would see in today's laws his worst fears, or even worse. Thus, my proposed revisions are submitted in a spirit of overdue reformation, in the prayer that checks and balances are still well enough in place for an orderly constitutional change that will bless all people. This proposal hopefully serves as a starting point for discussion will be seen as a simple effort to support such checks and balances.

The real issue at the federal level is with the laws, not the Constitution. But by the same token, the language of the Constitution is antiquated in syntax and spellings and certain details, and it was a rushed document as Benjamin Franklin refused to allow the adjournment of the Constitutional Convention until it was produced. In this proposal, I add language consistent with the six pillars, and also incorporate all its Amendments into the body of the text – a desirable but unattainable goal in 1787 for the original amendments.

Finally, the pattern here following the structure in the proposed revisions of the Connecticut Constitution and Statutes should be apparent. Also, at both the state and federal levels I have found it necessary to be explicit in the definition of human life and marriage. These realities were readily assumed in the eighteenth century, but with recent social upheavals and the creeping lawlessness of new legalisms, these concerns now need explicit definition.

The United States Constitution and General Laws

(Proposed Revision © 2012 John C. Rankin)

Preamble

We the people of the United States of America, in order to establish a just, peaceful and prosperous nation, and defense of the same, establish this Constitution and General Laws.

We make six assumptions that serve the consent of the governed, and thus an honest political union.

First, the unalienable rights of life, liberty and property, given by the Creator, belong to all people equally, and leaders in human government honor such rights.

Second, leaders in human government are to be fully transparent in all manners related to the public trust.

Third, an honest definition of terms in necessary in human government, providing a level playing field for all ideas to be heard equally, apart from which political freedom is not possible.

Fourth, leaders in human government are to honor and answer those who pose them the toughest questions.

Fifth, leaders in human government are to respect the common humanity of even the harshest of political opponents.

Sixth, in the face of our individual and societal transgressions against each other, leaders in human government are to work toward justice and reconciliation.

We embrace limited government with built in checks and balances, where the goal is to devolve governing responsibilities to the several states and then to the most local level possible, and where simplicity and truth are seen as partners. Accordingly, the maximum discretion of private citizens to organize their social space benefits society the best.

Article I
The Bill of Rights

Section 1:1: The unalienable rights of life, liberty and property belong to all people equally under the rule of law. The first order of human government is to protect human life for its entire natural duration, out of which liberty and property rights become possible. This priority is based on the social compact of the marriage of one man and woman in mutual fidelity, insofar as attainable, and on the fullest presence possible of both father and mother in the raising of children.

Section 1:2: Religious liberty is the first freedom, where the state cannot define religion, nor can any religious group define the state. Then there follows the freedoms of speech, the press, peaceable assembly, and the power of the people to petition the government for a redress of grievances.

Section 1:3: A well-regulated militia, being necessary to the security of a free people, and the right of the people to keep and bear arms, is affirmed. No soldier, in time of peace, may be quartered in any house without the consent of the owner or resident, or in time of war, but only in a manner prescribed by law.

Section 1:4: The people have the right to be secure in their persons, houses, papers, communications and effects, against unreasonable searches and seizures, by any means. No warrants are issued except for probable cause, supported by oath or affirmation, with specificity describing the place to be searched, and the persons or things to be seized. Privacy rights exist where a) the substance is original with the person and does not interfere with the life, liberty or property of others, b) protection for the innocent in criminal matters, and c) when national defense against enemies without or within is needful.

Section 1:5: No person can be held to answer for a capital or otherwise infamous crime unless indicted by a Grand Jury, and holds exemption during actual service in time of war or public danger. No person can be subject to the same offense twice, being put in jeopardy of life or limb. No person can be compelled in any criminal case to be a witness against himself. No person may be deprived of life, liberty or property, without due process of law. No private property can be taken for the public trust as specified in law without just compensation.

Section 1:6: In all criminal prosecutions, the accused enjoys the right to a speedy and public trial, by an impartial jury of the state and district where the crime, as charged, was committed, and with the district being previously defined by law. The accused is informed of the nature and cause of the accusation, is confronted by the witnesses against him, has compulsory process for obtaining witnesses in his favor, and has the assistance of counsel for his defense.

Section 1:7: In suits at common law, the right of trial by jury is preserved, and no fact tried by a jury will otherwise be re-examined in any Court of the United States, other than according to the rules of the common law. Excessive bail cannot be required, nor excessive fines imposed, nor cruel and unusual punishments inflicted.

Section 1:8: The constitutional definition of specific rights cannot be used to deny or disparage other rights enjoyed by the people. Those powers not specifically delegated to the United States by the Constitution, nor prohibited by it to the states, belong to the states and ultimately to the people.

Section 1:9: All persons who are legally born or naturalized in the United States, and subject to its jurisdiction, are citizens of the United States and of the state in which they reside. They are free to register to vote upon the age of eighteen years, which equals majority age unless otherwise stipulated by law. This freedom may not be abridged or denied unless they have participated in rebellion or other crimes.

Article II
Checks and Balances on Power

Section 2:1: The United States is a federation of the several states, and it powers are limited to those defined in this Constitution and General Laws.

Section 2:2: There are checks and balances on power within the federal government, consisting of three separate divisions, each with their own jurisdiction – the Legislative, the Executive and the Judicial. The Legislative, on its own terms, may delegate regulatory authority to the Executive.

Section 2:3: The Congress adopts laws, or repeals the same, requiring a two-thirds vote. Or it may adopt directives, of 100 words or less, by a simple majority vote, submitted by the executive, or federal departments responsible for their enforcement. All directives are by definition subcategories of laws, and may likewise be repealed.

Section 2:4: The Judiciary only decides matters before it according to constitutional language and scope.

Article III
The Legislative

Section 3:1: All legislative powers are vested in a Congress of the United States, which consists of a House of Representatives and Senate. All bills are for integral purpose, and only voted on as a whole, without amendment.

Section 3:2: The House of Representatives of the United States is composed of members chosen every even-numbered second year from each state.

A person qualified to serve as a Representative is at least 25 years of age, has been a citizen of the United States for seven years, and resides in the state in which he is elected. Representatives are apportioned among the several states according to the number of citizens recorded in the decennial census.

Every state has at least one Representative, and when vacancies occur, the executive authority of the state will call an election to choose a replacement. The House of Representatives chooses its own Speaker and other officers, and has the sole power of impeachment.

Section 3:3: All bills for revenue originate in the House of Representatives, and the Senate may propose or concur in joint committee as with other bills.

Every bill as passed by the House and Senate is presented to the President of the United States, and becomes law upon his signature. If he chooses to return it to the House stating his objections, they may reconsider and resubmit the bill together with the Senate, by a roll call vote. If the President still objects, and this process between the Legislative and Executive remains at an impasse, the House and Senate, by a two-thirds vote, may enact a bill into law without the President's signature. If upon receipt of a bill, the President does not return the bill with his signature within ten days, it becomes law, unless Congress, by means of adjournment, precludes such a timetable. This same process applies to any order or resolution requiring the concurrence of the House and Senate.

Section 3:4: The Senate of the United States is composed of two Senators from each state, elected every six years by its voters, with one-third of the seats up for election every other even-numbered year. It has the same electoral criteria as that of the House of Representatives, including the matter of vacancies, except that a Senator must be thirty years of age and a citizen of the United States for nine years. When a vacancy occurs in the Senate, the executive authority of the state calls for an election to fill the vacancy, or the legislature of the state may empower the executive to fill the vacancy as they direct.

The Vice President of the United States is the President of the Senate, and exercises a vote only when necessary to break a tie. The Senate chooses its own Speaker and other officers, and a President pro tempore in the absence of the Vice President, or when he must exercise the office of the President of the United States.

The Senate has the sole power to try all impeachments for members of the executive and judicial branches, for reasons of treason, bribery or other high crimes or misdemeanors, and when sitting for that purpose, does so by oath or affirmation. When the President of the United States is tried, the Chief Justice of the Supreme Court presides, and no person is convicted except for a vote of two-thirds of the members present. Judgments in cases of impeachment extend no further than removal from office and disqualification to hold any office of honor, trust or profit under the United States. But liability remains subject to indictment, trial, judgment and punishment according to law.

Section 3:5: The oversight for the elections of Representatives and Senators is prescribed by the State Legislatures, subject to the laws of the United States Congress.

The Congress assembles every year beginning at noon on the first weekday following January 1st, with the terms of the prior Congress ending at the same time following the most recent election. The timetable for the same, for the President and Vice President, is at noon three weeks following in January.

Section 3:6: Each House has full oversight concerning elections, returns, qualifications of its own members, rules of proceedings, and the power to expel a member based on a two-thirds vote. A majority of each constitutes a quorum, but a ten percent is authorized to compel the attendance of absent members as it determines.

Neither House, during the session of Congress, without the consent of the other, will adjourn for more than three days, nor to any place except the Capitol Building, excepting states of emergency.

Section 3:7: The Congress defines its own rules, protocols and enforcements, appoints its own officers, counsel and committees, employs those necessary, oversees elections, and delegates duties to the federal departments responsible for particular oversight and enforcement. The Congress sets the terms for compensation and expenses for its members, as paid by the U.S. Treasury, by a roll call vote of no less than a two-thirds majority, taking effect no sooner than the commencement of the next Congress. They may pass no laws for their own compensation and benefits that exempts them as a special class. They are free from arrest during the session, including transport to and from, except for treason, felony and breach of peace. For any speech or debate they make in either House, they are not to be held liable in any other place. All contracts with public or private concerns are made in open meetings, including all bidding processes, and with full access to the media.

No Representative or Senator during time of service will be appointed to any other civil office in the United States, or receive any extra financial benefits related to his service. And no person holding any office under the United States will at the same time be a member of either House.

Section 3:8: The Congress alone has the power to lay and collect taxes, duties, tolls, fees and excises in a nationally uniform standard, to pay the debts and provide for the common defense and general welfare of the United States. All taxes, duties, tolls, fees and excises must be in fair proportion to government's legitimate needs, must be derived from productive economic activity, and must encourage entrepreneurial ventures and capital formation for businesses and job creation.

The Congress may:

Borrow money on the credit of the United States; regulate commerce with foreign nations, among the several states and with the Indian tribes; establish post offices and interstate roads; establish a uniform rule of naturalization, and uniform laws on the subject on bankruptcies;

Coin money and regulate its value backed by gold reserves, regulate the use of foreign coin, fix the standard of weights and measures, and provide for punishment of counterfeiting the securities and current coin of the United States;

Promote the progress of science and useful arts by securing for limited times to authors and inventors the exclusive right to their respective writings and discoveries, insofar as the same are in accord with the given natural order;

Constitute tribunals inferior to the Supreme Court; define and punish piracies and felonies committed on the high seas, and offenses against the laws of nations;

Declare war, grant letters of marque and reprisal, and make rules concerning captures on land and water; raise and support armies, but no appropriation of money for such use exceeds two years; provide for an army, navy, marines, air force and other military services deemed needful; make rules governing all the military services; provide for the calling and discipline of the militia to serve the regular armed forces as necessary, reserving to the states respectively the appointment of officers and authority for training the militia.

Exercise exclusive legislation in all cases in the District of Columbia as the seat of the United States Government, which does not exceed ten square miles, with all necessary buildings and resources; and

Make all laws necessary and proper for executing the foregoing powers, and all other powers vested by this Constitution in the Government of the United States, or in any of its departments.

Section 3:9: The Congress maintains a website and publishes all its proceedings on a daily basis, with ample advance notice for any interested citizen, and publishes the same in print.

Section 3:10: The Congress must balance its budget every fiscal year, and defining the dates of its fiscal year as it sees fit. The Congress oversees the Library of Congress, and also the Postal Service. No member of Congress is to serve as a member of any jury, petit or grand, within the United States, while in office.

Section 3:11: Members of Congress are elected in each state on the first Tuesday after November 1, biennially on even numbered years for all Representatives, and one-third of Senators. Replacements for vacancies that occur mid-term are filled by the several states and territories. Members of Congress thus chosen are certified by the state's chief executive, countersigned by the Secretary of State, and begin their term on the first weekday following the next January 1st.

Section 3:12: Representative districts are the most naturally defined and contiguous territory radiating from the heaviest population center, and as reasonably equal in population with all other districts as such natural boundaries accord, never splitting any municipality insofar as possible, and never splitting precincts. At the decennial census districts are reapportioned accordingly.

Section 3:13: None of the several states may usurp any of these enumerated prerogatives of the Congress.

None of the several states, without the consent of the Congress, lays any duties on imports or exports except what is absolutely necessary for executing its inspection laws. The net produce of all duties laid by any state is for the use of the United States Treasury, with all such laws subject to revision and control of the Congress.

None of the several states, without the consent of the Congress, lays any duty of tonnage, keeps troops or ships of war in times of peace, enters into any agreement or compact with another state or foreign power, or engages in war, unless actually invaded, or in imminent and unavoidable danger.

Section 3:14: The privilege of the writ of habeas corpus is not suspended except when cases of rebellion, invasion or public safety require it.

No bill of attainder or ex post facto law is passed; no poll tax or other direct tax on income is levied, or any levy placed on any articles exported from any state; and the right of citizens to vote may not be abridged or denied by reason of failure to pay any tax.

No preference is given by any regulation of commerce favoring the ports of one state over another, nor are any vessels in interstate commerce obligated to pay duties to another state.

No monies are drawn from the Treasury except due to appropriations made by law. A regular statement of account for receipts and expenditures is made and published periodically, and always available concurrently on the U.S Government's website.

No title of nobility is granted in the United States, and no person holding any office of profit or trust under them accepts any present, compensation, office or title of any kind from any foreign state or leaders therein.

Section 3:15: The Congress has the power to dispose of and make all needful rules and regulations respecting the territory or other property belonging to the United States. Nothing in this Constitution is construed so as to prejudice any claims of the United States or of any particular state.

Section 3:16: The United States guarantees to every state in the Union a republican form of government, and protects each of them against invasion, or against domestic violence as requested by the state legislature, or of the executive when the legislature cannot be convened.

Section 3:17: Full faith and credit is given in each state to the public acts, records and judicial proceedings of every other state. The Congress through general laws may prescribe the manner in which such acts, records and proceedings are proved, and their effects.

Section 3:18: The citizens of the United States are entitled to all the privileges and immunities of citizens in the several states. A person charged with treason, felony or other crime, flees from justice and is found in another state, is on demand of the executive authority of the state from which he fled, to be returned to the state having jurisdiction of the crime.

Section 3:19: New states may be admitted by Congress into the Union, provided that no new state is formed or erected within the jurisdiction of another state, nor formed by the junction of two or more states or parts of states, or without the consent of the legislatures of the states concerned as well as that of the Congress.

Section 3:20: This Constitution, and the laws of the United States that are made in its pursuance, and all treaties made under the authority of the United States, are the supreme law of the land. Judges in every state are thus bound, notwithstanding anything in the state constitutions to the contrary.

Section 3:21: The Representatives and Senators of the Congress, the members of the legislatures of the several states, and all executive and judicial officers, both of the United States and of the several states, will be bound by oath or affirmation to support this Constitution. No religious test is ever required as a qualification to any office or public trust under the United States.

Any person elected, appointed or otherwise hired to serve any position or job, employed or subcontracted, in the United States Government, will state publicly in the presence of the most senior duly authorized agent of the United States appropriate and available, unless otherwise specifically stated, the following: "I solemnly swear (or affirm), in service to the Constitution of the United States, in all honesty and faithfulness, and to the best of my abilities, to discharge all my assigned responsibilities with impartiality, so help me God" (this last clause being optional).

Section 3:22: No person may serve in any office of public trust in the United States if he has participated in insurrection or rebellion against the same, unless permitted by two-thirds of each House. No public debt or obligation may be assumed by the United States or any state incurred in the aid of insurrection or rebellion against the United States. No state, without its consent, is deprived of its equal suffrage in the Senate.

Section 3:23: The Congress, whenever two-thirds of both Houses deem it necessary, proposes amendments to this Constitution. Or the legislatures of two-thirds of the several states may call a convention for the same. In either case, the Constitution is only amended when ratified by three-fourths of the several states.

Article IV
The Executive

Section 4:1: The executive power is vested in a President of the United States of America. He holds his office for four years, and can serve no more than two and a half terms. As chief executive officer of the nation, the President has sole discretion, oversight and the power of delegation on all matters pertaining to his office, and decides which department heads will serve in his cabinet. His contracts with public or private concerns, apart from matters of national security, are made in open meetings, including all bidding processes, and with full access to the media.

Section 4:2: No person except a natural born citizen of the United States is eligible to serve as President, nor any person who is not at least thirty-five years of age and a resident of the United States for at least fourteen years.

Section 4:3: The President's compensation is set by the Congress, taking effect no sooner than the beginning of the next term in office, and is afforded by Congress the protection by the Secret Service and a White House police staff. The President receives no other compensation during this period from the United States or any of the several states.

Section 4:4: Together with the Vice President, he is chosen accordingly:

Each state legislature appoints an electoral college equal to the number of its Senators and Representatives in the Congress, with no member of Congress or other person holding an office of trust or profit under the United States eligible as an elector. The District of Columbia, as the seat of the United States government, is entitled to its electors, and not being a state, has no more electors than that entitled to the least populous state.

The electors meet in their respective states and vote by individual ballot each for the President and Vice President, both of whom reside in different states. They then sign, certify and transmit the ballots under seal to the seat of the United States government, directed by the President of the Senate. The Congress may determine a nationally uniform date for choosing the electors.

In the presence of the Senate and House of Representatives assembled, the certificates are opened and votes tallied, and the person having the majority number of votes for President is elected. If no majority is attained, then the House of Representatives chooses the President immediately by ballot from among the top three vote getters, where each State has one vote, decided by a majority of its own electors. A quorum equals two-thirds of the states, and a majority of all the states is necessary to make the choice. The House may not adjourn until the selection is made, regardless of how many ballots are required. If the President-elect dies before being sworn into office, the Vice President-elect becomes President.

Section 4:5: Before the President enters the execution of his office, he takes the following oath of affirmation: "I do solemnly swear (or affirm) that I will faithfully execute the Office of President of the United States, and will to the best of my ability, preserve, protect and defend the Constitution of the United States, so help me God (this last clause being optional).

In the case of the removal of the President by death or resignation, the Vice President becomes President. When there is a vacancy in the office of the Vice President, the President nominates a Vice President who takes office upon a majority vote of both Houses of Congress.

The President, Vice President and all civil officers of the United States are to be removed from office on impeachment for and conviction of treason, bribery or other high crimes or misdemeanors.

Whenever the President declares in writing to the President pro tempore of the Senate, and the Speaker of the House of Representatives, that he is unable to discharge the powers and duties of his office for a season, such powers and duties are discharged by the Vice President as Acting President.

Whenever the Vice President and a majority of either the secretaries of the federal departments, or another body as the Congress may provide by law, declare in writing by the protocol above that the President is unable to discharge the powers and duties of his office, the Vice President immediately assumes the office as Acting President.

If the President challenges this action by means of the same protocol, he resumes his power and duties of office unless within four days the Vice President re-sustains his action. Then the Congress assembles immediately, within forty-eight hours if not in session, and decides the issue within twenty-one days by a two-thirds vote.

Section 4:6: The President is the Commander in Chief of the Army, Navy, Marines and Air Force of the United States, and of the militia of the several states when called into actual service of the United States.

Section 4:7: The Chief Joints of Staff is composed of a chairman, from among the chief officers of the regular components of the armed services, serving as the chief adviser to the President and Secretary of Defense, and a vice-chairman appointed by the President from the same pool, along with the Chief of Staff of the Army, the Chief of Naval Operations, the Chief of Staff of the Air Force and the Commandant of the Marines.

The Secretary of Defense is a civilian appointed by the President, with the advice and consent of the Senate, is responsible for all aspects in oversight of the Department of Defense in service to the well being of the nation and all military personnel, and stewards an official seal for his office. There is a Uniform Code of Military Justice set by the Secretary of Defense in conjunction with the Chief Joints of Staff.

The Secretary of the Army serves under the direction of the Secretary of Defense, is a civilian appointed by the President, with the advice and consent of the Senate, and is responsible for all aspects in oversight of the Army, including the U.S. Army Corps of Engineers, and stewards an official seal for his office.

The Secretary of the Navy serves under the direction of the Secretary of Defense, is a civilian appointed by the President, with the advice and consent of the Senate, and is responsible for all aspects in oversight of the Navy, Marine Corps and Coast Guard, and stewards an official seal for his office, and stewards an official seal for his office.

The Secretary of the Air Force serves under the direction of the Secretary of Defense, is a civilian appointed by the President, with the advice and consent of the Senate, and is responsible for all aspects in oversight of the Air Force, and stewards an official seal for his office.

Section 4:8: The compensation for those who serve in the Armed Forces is designed to serve the family unit in the face of their duties, and the care for veterans is likewise designed to be honorable and comprehensive.

The U.S. Armed Services is a voluntary force, apart from Congressional override in a time of national emergency. Upon enlistment, all new recruits publicly state before any designated commissioned officer of any armed force: " I, _____, do solemnly swear (or affirm) that I will support and defend the Constitution of the United States against all enemies, foreign and domestic; that I will bear true faith and allegiance to the same; and that I will obey the orders of the President of the United States and the orders of the officers appointed over me, according to regulations and the Uniform Code of Military Justice; so help me God" (this last clause is optional).

Section 4:9: The President may make executive orders consistent with the prerogative of his office and in accord with constitutional law, may make policy directives consistent with its constitutional provision, may require the opinion, in writing, of the secretaries of all federal departments relative to their duties, and has the power to grant reprieves and pardons for offenses against the United States, except in cases of impeachment.

The President has the power to make treaties, with the advice and consent of two-thirds of the Senate. He likewise nominates and appoints ambassadors, other public ministers and consuls, judges of the Supreme Court, and all other officers of the United States whose appointments are not otherwise provided for. By law, the Congress may give authority to such inferior officers as they think proper, in the President alone, in the courts of law or in the heads of departments.

The President has the power to fill vacancies that may occur during an officially declared recess of the Senate, granting commissions that expire at the end of the next session.

Section 4:10: The President, from time to time, gives to the Congress information on the state of the Union, and recommends for their consideration such measures as he judges necessary and expedient. On extraordinary occasions, he may convene both Houses, or either of them, and in the case of disagreement between them, may adjourn them to such time he thinks proper. He receives ambassadors and other public ministers, takes care that the laws be faithfully executed, and commissions all the officers of the United States.

Section 4:11: The President has the authority to establish and oversee a Committee on Political Ideas (COPI), solely, or in delegation to or in conjunction with the initiative of the Senate, which also has sole initiative power. Its purpose is to be sure all ideas for political debate are discussed in a public and open-ended fashion. COPI has no lawmaking power, but serves as a resource for lawmakers. On a given topic, COPI receives applications from partisans, prioritizes their testimonies, and works through them until all ideas have been fully and publically aired. Written presentations for COPI are a maximum 2,000 words, presented orally, there is no limit on annotation and attachments, and are followed by open-ended dialogue in all directions until the partisan is satisfied that he has been fully heard.

Article V
The Judicial

Section 5:1: The judicial power of the United States is vested in one Supreme Court, and in such inferior courts as the Congress time to time may ordain and establish. The Supreme Court is the final arbiter of all contested federal legal matters, and is bound by specific oath and affirmation to the Constitution consistent with Article III, Section 21. They receive for their services compensation that is not diminished during their continuance in office.

Section 5:2: The members of the Supreme Court are nine in total, and nominated by the President with the advice and consent of the Senate. All members of the lower federal courts are likewise nominated and ratified, with their jurisdictions and numbers determined by law. All federal judges may be questioned by the U.S. Congress in public hearings if two-thirds of both Houses consent. The President may request of the Supreme Court a non-binding opinion in writing on a point of his concern. And members of the Supreme Court may be impeached and removed by three-quarters of the Congress in joint session. All contracts with public or private concerns are made in open meetings, including all bidding processes, and with full access to the media.

Section 5:3: In all cases affecting ambassadors other public ministers and consuls, and those in which a state is a party, the Supreme Court has original jurisdiction. In all other cases, the Supreme Court has original jurisdiction, both as to law and fact, except under regulations as Congress may make.

Section 5:4: The judges, both of the supreme and inferior courts, hold their offices during good behavior in service to the Constitution, and are subject to recall by a vote of three-fourths of the Congress.

Section 5:5: The trial of all crimes except in cases of impeachment, are by jury. Such trial occurs in the state where the crimes are alleged to have been committed. When not committed within any state, the trial will be at such place as the Congress by law directs.

Section 5:6: Treason against the United States consists only in levying war against them, or in giving their enemies aid and comfort. No person may be convicted of treason apart from the testimony of two witnesses to the same overt act, or in confession in open court. Congress has the power to declare the punishment for treason, but no attainder of treason may work corruption of blood for forfeiture during the life of the person disgraced.

Section 5:7: For matters involving federal jurisdiction, there is a system of federal Common Courts in each of the several states, where power is vested in committees of common judges. There are seven members in each committee, elected statewide every two years, with as many such committees as each state sees fit. The rules of procedure are set by the same. These committees have the power, in non-felonious matters, and upon the written consent of all parties to a given complaint, to resolve issues so that they need not go through the regular federal court system. The location for the complaint is the state of the defendant's residency or business, the committees of common judges guarantee a public hearing and resolution within six weeks of filing, with all decisions being final, and with no appeals in the regular federal courts.

Article VI
General Laws

Section 6:1: All terms used in this Constitution and General Laws are understood according to the plain meaning of normal English usage and specific context. The use of the male pronoun is gender inclusive unless otherwise indicated. If there is a disagreement between parties concerning the definition and applicability of a particular term, it is to be resolved ahead of usage, in a) U.S. Common Court, b) Regular Court, or c) legislative debate in the United States Congress.

Section 6:2: Any person who knowingly provides false information on any document he or she signs, in private contracts or in government business, is liable for immediate loss of related privilege, and for penalties as assessed in Common Court or the Regular Courts. Any person who deliberately subverts public order in any capacity is guilty of a felony.

Section 6:3: The executive, legislative and judicial branches of the government may grant access to privately funded chaplains for the express service to employees who desire the same. Any religious or non-religious organization has the freedom to hire such chaplains, so long as their organizations support unalienable rights under due process of law.

Section 6:4: Legal holidays, where all public institutions are closed except for emergency personnel, include: New Year's Day (January 1); Martin Luther King Day (the first Monday on or after January 15); President's Day (the third Monday in February); Memorial Day (the last Monday in May); Independence Day (July 4); Labor Day (the first Monday in September); Columbus Day (the second Monday in October); Veterans Day (November 11); Thanksgiving Day (the fourth Thursday of November); and Christmas Day (December 25); the President may also issue a call for a special holiday, and as approved by the Congress.

Section 6:5: If any private or governmental contractual obligation or constitutional requirement falls on a Sunday or a legal holiday, or religiously required holiday, the next day or next business day suffices as the deadline.

Section 6:6: The standard time for the nation is rooted in the District of Columbia, equals the seventy-fifth meridian west of Greenwich; it is modified at 2:00 a.m. in advance by one hour on the second Sunday in March, until 2:00 a.m. on the first Sunday of November.

Section 6:7: There are three types of legal contracts for all federal business – two forms of "open contract" and one form of a "closed contract." An open contract must be on one side of a standard 8 ½ x11 piece of paper, and if "simple," it has a maximum of fifty words in the body of the text. If "regular," it has a maximum of 300 words in the body of the text. A closed contract is not thus limited. At the top of all contracts the following disclosure is required, and to be immediately signed and dated underneath by the agreeing parties: "This contract is either a simple open contract [ ], a regular open contract [ ] or a closed contract [ ], according to the laws of the United States – check only one box to the right." All disputes concerning open contracts are adjudicated only in the Common Courts.

Section 6:8: All candidates for federal public office must maintain an official campaign website. They are to disclose donor names with current postal addresses, with amount given, immediately. There is no limit to monies that can be given, and all such candidates are bound by Article V, Section 2, and its enforcements insofar as their campaigns may neither promise nor solicit special benefit. No monies may be solicited from non U.S. citizens, and to do so is a felony. Any such monies received without solicitation are to be publicly identified and placed in the public treasury.

Section 6:9: All citizens are free to lobby federal public officials as individuals or as groups, for matters in which they have interest, spending monies as necessary, but contributions to political candidates may only be made by individual United States citizens, as individuals. Public officials are accountable to the legal scrutiny of any elector, group of electors or public officials, if evidence is presented in court that they have engaged in promise or delivery of goods or services that constitute special benefit, and they are thus held liable if convicted.

Section 6:10: All meetings designated public by federal departments and/or public officials are open to all, are accountable to public inquiry and commentary, announced with ample advance notice on appropriate websites and by other means, apart from emergency meetings voted on by the Congress in accord with the privacy rights in Article 1, Section 4.

Section 6:11: All public meetings may be fully recorded in any fashion, given reasonable accommodation. The content and details for all meetings and communications among public officials are fully available to any elector in any medium recorded by the public officials, as soon as practicable.

Section 6:12: The Flag of the United States, composed of the historic stars and stripes in red, white and blue, with one star representing each state, is to be treated with respect as a symbol of a free people, and is suitable for display on all appropriate occasions.

Section 6:13: The Pledge of Allegiance is voluntary in nature and is composed of these words: "I pledge allegiance to the flag of the United States of America and to the Republic for which it stands, one Nation, under God, indivisible, with liberty and justice for all," and is suitable for any and all public purposes.

Section 6:14: The Great Seal of the United States is composed minimally of the historic representation of the American bald eagle, with the thirteen arrows in one claw, the olive branch in the other, the escutcheon on the breast, and scroll in its beak with the words, "E Pluribus Unum," and is suitable for any and all governmental purposes.

Section 6:15: The authority of the U.S. Government is limited to those powers delegated to it by the several states, only as necessary for the cooperation of the several states as federated for the well being of the nation as a whole. It spends no tax revenues for any purposes wholly within the scope and geography of state or local jurisdictions.

Section 6:16: Along with detailed and current information provided on the federal government's website relative to their public functions, all federal public legislators and officials must maintain a personal and current website giving full transparency to the interface of their public and private interests, in both cases with simple access, concomitant with Article V, Section 2. They are free to conduct business, relative to which their participation in public life grants them no special benefit, unless otherwise stipulated by law. Where a conflict of interest may arise, the public official is to disclose all such concerns in specificity, so that the people may monitor any potential cause for conflict. If the public official is charged with and found guilty of using his office for special benefit and/or personal gain, it is a felony, he will also be liable for immediate removal from office or position, a minimum ten-year ban from subsequent public office or position, a minimum of treble monetary damages, payable as the courts may decide, and other penalties as the courts may decide. The same rules apply when the public official leaves office, relative to his time of service.

Article VII
Federal Departments

Section 7:1: Each federal department has a Secretary as head, appointed by the President, and is subject to approval or removal by the Senate. He sets policy directives consistent with the Constitution and oversight of the Congress, maintains a current website with all matters disclosed in full that do not fall under the scope of protected constitutional privacy rights, serving respectively as executive officers and stewards of their respective seals.

Section 7:2: When a department head cannot continue to serve, temporarily or permanently, the President will appoint an acting head, and nominate a new head within thirty days.

Section 7:3: Each department has its own budget, and is responsible for setting any and all appropriate fees for service, subject to approval by the Congress. All contracts with public or private concerns are made in open meetings, including all bidding processes, and with full access to the media.

Section 7:4: The Department of Administration has a Secretary as its head who is responsible for all aspects of oversight concerning staff planning, budgeting and necessary coordination for all departments of the federal government, and for administering all aspects of personnel policy and material provisions for all departments.

Section 7:5: The Department of Justice is headed by the Attorney General who is appointed by the President with the advice and consent of the Senate, as are all United States Attorneys and other executive officers as determined by law. The Attorney General appoints Assistant Attorneys General as needful, and represents the executive branch in all litigation matters except where there is a conflict of interest, recusing himself in favor of an Assistant Attorney General. He represents the United States government as a whole, oversees the organization of the federal courts, and delegates authority to lesser offices.

Section 7:6: The Department of State has a Secretary as its head who is appointed by the President with the advice and consent of the Senate, and is responsible for all aspects of oversight concerning foreign relations and immigration, and wherever religious, political and economic liberties are respected or sought after in foreign lands, the United States is free to join in mutually appropriate relationships.

The United States maintains its prerogative for national sovereignty and defense as the best means to be an agent for religious, political and economic liberty within the community of nations, respecting equally the same aspirations of all other peoples.

The United States interferes in no internal matters of other sovereign nations, whether free or otherwise, only acting on matters of defense against the designs of other nations or other hostile groups against the sovereignty and freedoms of the United States, and only to the extent of protection of the same.

As recommended by the President and implemented by the State Department, the United States ranks every foreign power on a sliding scale of how well it serves religious, political and economic liberty for its peoples. A ranking of ten equals complete liberty, a ranking of zero equals complete enslavement. The United States must rank itself by the exact same criteria before it does so for any foreign power.

The United States maintains diplomatic relations with all free nations. With respect to any foreign power where freedom lacks, the United States is free to have restricted or no diplomatic relations. All American citizens who travel, live in or do business with nations where the United States has restricted or no diplomatic relations, do so on their own recognizance and risk.

The Department of State issues and sets standards for U.S. passports. Immigration policy is rooted in the identity of the United States as a nation of immigrants, and continues in the same spirit as protected by the rule of law.

Section 7:7: The Department of Domestic Security has a Secretary as its head who oversees and delegates all aspects of necessary coordination in civil matters of protecting the security of the nation from threats without and within, for protecting the national borders from illegal entry of aliens, and for an orderly immigration policy that serves the national interest. The Secretary is accountable to the President and the Secretary of Defense in overseeing all matters of intelligence as an integrated whole.

All aliens in the country legally have their unalienable rights protected. Aliens in the country illegally are guaranteed their life, liberty and property according to due process of law as they face any and all processes that holds them accountable for illegal entry.

Section 7:8: The Department of Elections has a Secretary as its head who oversees and delegates all aspects of federal elections, ensuring integrity and the inviolate freedom to vote of all qualified electors, and for conducting the decennial census.

Section 7:9: The Department of the Treasury has a Secretary as its head who is responsible for oversight in all matters of regulation of the national currency, national banks, bankruptcy regulations, the collection of taxes and fees due the United States, enforcement of the same, and of the issuing, when necessary, of bonds, and oversees the Secret Service; all in service to a free market economy. The Secretary posts the nation's finances daily on his official website.

Taxes for the operation of the United States government are collected only by means of a) a federal sales tax, and b) fees for service as approved by the Congress. The sales tax is uniform and collected on all goods sold in the nation or its territories, or leases other than for primary residence. It is reported and paid by businesses on a weekly basis, or by individuals on a monthly basis. Exempted goods are primary personal needs in matters of rent, food, clothing and medicine. The percentage figure for the federal sales tax is determined by the Congress in due proportion, each year, relative to budgetary needs, after a balanced budget is passed.

If revenues exceed the budget by up to twenty percent, those monies are to be set aside in a publicly viewable bank account for emergency use as determined by a two-thirds vote of each House of the Congress, returnable to the general budget relative to subsequent revenue deficits that may occur within the fiscal year. For revenues that exceed the twenty percent overage, they are to be set aside in another publicly viewable bank account, to be applied to the subsequent year's budget before the tax percentage for that year is calculated.

Any person charged with and convicted of deliberate tax fraud is guilty of a federal felony. Any revenues produced on federally recognized Indian reservations are at their discretion, so long as there is no violation of federal and state civil rights. The Department of the Treasury has the power to make laws to control traffic access from federal highways and lands to and from Indian reservations, assessing tolls as deemed necessary for the well being of the Union.

Section 7:10: The Department of Health has a Secretary as its head who oversees and delegates all aspects of necessary coordination between the states in matters of health safety, ensuring uniform standards for the nation.

Section 7:11: The Department of Food and Drugs has a Secretary as its head who is responsible for oversight in assuring uniform standards of food quality and drug safety, and enforcement of the same.

All food, medicine and clothing sold in the United States, regardless of origin, will carry a simple, prominent and easy to read label, with the applicable category or categories being checked off: all natural [ ]; natural with some synthetic additions [ ]; synthetic with some natural elements [ ]; all synthetic [ ]; contains genetically modified organisms (GMOs). All ingredients are likewise to be listed in a suitable place, with clear and simple delineation of benefits and risks for food, food supplements, medicine and GMOs.

The legal age for the purchase and public use of alcoholic beverages is 21. Those who abuse themselves by means of alcohol, nicotine, other controlled substances or illegal substances, and do not harm the life, liberty or property of another person, pay the penalty in their own persons, and are not to be penalized more than for a misdemeanor. They have no legal right to impose themselves upon others for remedy, but private agencies dedicated to charity on their behalf may offer such help.

The illegal sale of alcohol, controlled substances, and illegal substances, where there is no resulting deprivation of life, liberty or property caused to any other person, does not merit incarceration, only fines as determined by law and/or suspension or revocation of U.S. passport.

Section 7:12: The Department of Commerce and Labor has a Secretary as its head who is responsible for all aspects in oversight of the coordination of all business relationships between the federal government and the states, between the states themselves, for organized labor and private entities, and in banking transparency. The Secretary always prefers to contract with businesses headquartered or located in the United States if skill, quality and cost are competitive. All federal contracts are open contracts unless the Congress makes exception by a two-thirds vote, to then be entered as a specific rule with the Department.

The Secretary sets standards for public and private corporations or associations doing business within its purview, including truth in advertising.

All professional and occupational licensing standards are set by the respective private accrediting agencies. Lacking such, the Congress may create its own. The Secretary determines to whom to issue licenses for doing business in its purview, and the procedure for application.

The Secretary oversees the rights of organized labor, including transparency in accountability to its members and the right to secret ballot in all elections. No person can be compelled to work on a day they announce ahead of time as their religiously defined weekly day of rest.

The Secretary oversees necessary coordination between the states and foreign powers in matters of commerce and trade, and sets all customs and duties, and as directed by Congress, assumes free market economy standards with all foreign powers that honor the same.

Section 7:13: The Department of Copyright and Patents has a Secretary as its head who oversees and delegates all aspects of standards for the copyright and patent of original works, which originate in the United States and its territories, whether material or intellectual in nature, and their time limits.

Section 7:14: The Department of Energy has a Secretary as its head who is responsible for all aspects of coordination among states and private companies concerning the well being of the energy supply for the nation, for overseeing national reserves, and for directives set by the President in times of national emergency.

Section 7:15: The Department of Agriculture has a Secretary as its head who oversees and delegates all aspects of necessary coordination between the states in matters of agricultural health and exports, commensurate to the service of a free market economy where no issues of life, liberty or property are at stake.

Section 7:16: The Department of Highways, Navigation and Transportation has a Secretary as its head who oversees all matters of the interstate and federal highway system, in coordination with the several states, all matters of navigation and navigable waters within federal jurisdiction, and in conjunction with the Coast Guard, and all matters of civil transportation on land and in the air, within federal jurisdiction.

Section 7:17: The Department of the United States Postal Service has a Secretary as its head who is responsible for oversight of a free market economy system of delivery of all letters and parcels within the United

States, and to and from other foreign places, guaranteeing to the citizenry a highly reliable and cost-effective system.

Section 7:18: The Department of Corrections has a Secretary as its head who is responsible for all aspects of oversight for administering the incarceration and remittance of those convicted of offenses under federal jurisdiction, for their reintegration into society, working with the several states accordingly. All inmates will be separated according to sex, minority versus majority age, and levels of offense, so that no harm will come to any inmate. For the conviction of committing even one sex crime while in prison, the offender will be remanded to a segregated place that removes the possibility for another such crime for the balance of the sentence. No pornographic or other material that dehumanizes people or abuses animals is allowed, and the Department may set other standards in conjunction with Congress.

Private chaplains are given appropriate access to minister to the needs of prisoners thus interested, and are accountable to affirm the unalienable rights for all people equally.

For women who give birth while in prison, the Department of Corrections will work with the respective state departments of Social Services, to define the best possible care for the children.

Section 7:19: The Department of Communications has a Secretary as its head who oversees all matters of coordination between the several states in matters of communications and the internet, commensurate to the service of a free market economy and federally protected public airwaves.

Section 7:20: The Department of Mining has a Secretary as its head who oversees all matters of mining safety, setting uniform national standards and enforcement of the same.

Section 7:21: The Department of Public Property and Ecology has a Secretary as its head who oversees all matters of the purchase, maintenance, and sale of federal properties, tangible or intangible. The Secretary also oversees all federal lands and parks not under military control, to ensure their public access and enjoyment congruent with sound ecological standards that preserve them appropriately in perpetuity, and to ensure the same ecological health for all waterways and air in the nation.

Section 7:22: The Department of Public Contracts and Printing has a Secretary as its head who oversees all matters of contracting and subcontracting for civil services from the private sector necessary for federal purposes, and all matters in printing public documents.

Those who work for the federal government are to be hired on no other basis but qualification to perform the job. They may choose to be a subcontractor or an employee. In either case, it is by open contract, and they are to be paid sufficiently well with total compensation being reasonably commensurate with the private sector, and subject to annual review. Collective bargaining is not permissible for federal workers.

Section 7:23: The Department of American Indian Tribes and Territories has a Secretary as its head who oversees all matters relating to recognized American Indian tribes, and administrative governance for U.S. territories and insular possessions. American Indian tribes are sovereign nations within the sovereign nation of the United States, and all American Indians are also United States citizens.

◆ ◆ ◆